OF
MEN
AND
CARS

by John Christy

ZIFF-DAVIS PUBLISHING COMPANY

NEW YORK

Library of Congress Catalogue Card Number 60-10521

Manufactured in the United States of America

Contents

Introduction

MAN AND MACHINE—two words and two entities that must function together. Without man the machine is an inanimate piece of metal, beautiful and well-conceived perhaps, but inanimate nonetheless. Without the machine, man is but a complicated biped, with all the limitations of the animal world. Put man and the machine together, however, and you have a combination that is almost invincible, a combination that can conquer worlds, and probably will.

There are all sorts of worlds. In an age when the goals of man and machine are the stars, it may seem old-fashioned to speak of land-bound efforts, but these are very special efforts. These are, for all their familiarity, very special men and very special machines. Without them, the stars would very likely have had to wait.

The world we speak of here is the world of speed; the men are the seekers of that world, and the machines are the means of attaining it. Their achievements have made a great difference in the lives of their fellow men. Without them, a man could not live in one place and work in another. There would be no suburbs, no shopping centers, no vacations in distant places; we would, most of us, live and die within a few short miles of where we were born.

These men of the world of speed are of all types. Some have contributed little; others have contributed much. Some have been merely content to use what others have created; others have been the builders. But without the users the builders would have had no reason to build, and so we can see that both groups have given the world much of themselves. Indeed, as you will see, some have given the ultimate gift.

For the most part, these are not men whose names are in the news, although some have been. In some instances their names and their cars are not even readily recalled to mind by the enthusiasts, but they are nonetheless important for that: in other instances their names and cars have become household words.

Here we have attempted to bring together a group of men whose exploits and achievements have made life easier and more enjoyable for all of us. More important, we have endeavored to entertain, for an evening or a day, those to whom a car means more than just a means of getting from point to point; those to whom being a "driver" means more than guiding with some skill and little talent a two-ton wheeled vehicle. Still more important, the authors of this book and the men of whom we write perhaps will have shown that even at this dawn of the age of space the wheel is not as yet an anachronism.

Part I

THE RECORD MEN:
Eternity Begins at Dawn

Of all the achievements by men with cars, none are more spectacular nor performed before a smaller audience than those of record setting, seeking the ultimate velocity at which a vehicle will carry a man over a given distance. This goal, by its very nature, requires open space and as few onlookers as possible.

Record setting is one of the most difficult and, at the same time, one of the easiest things to do with an automobile. Difficult because of the effort, brains, and money that must be poured into a vehicle that is designed to go as fast as possible for a time varying from a few seconds, over a measured mile, to several days over a 10-mile circle; easy because once you have achieved the vehicle it becomes merely a matter of expanding the courage and stamina required to hold it on course at the prescribed speed for the measured distance.

Faith must be added to courage; faith that the machine, which is a marvelous fabrication of thousands of parts, will stay in one piece during the stress and strain of the run. If this miracle is achieved you may have earned a record; if not, your reward may be disaster.

The record men are a breed unto themselves, yet they are not alike. The one thing they share in common is their dedication to a goal. Here are the stories of several such men, each a genius in his own way, yet as different from one another as men can possibly be.

1. Twelve Hours is Forever
by John Christy

Perhaps the most outstanding aspect of setting any sort of speed record is the element of strain. In the case of a long distance record another element is added—that of sheer suspense. Months have gone into the preparation of car and crew. Untold hours have been spent in transporting these men and machines to the point where the record attempt is to be made. Of necessity, the course must be in a remote area, probably far from the home base. Untold other hours must be spent trying to anticipate any mishap that might stop the attempt and in trying to provide the tools and material to cope with any, or almost any, eventuality.

Once the car and crew are at the record course and the first rap of exhaust barks in the chilled predawn air, the suspense and strain begin. There is nothing more that can be done; the car and driver start out, and you begin to wait. In an agony of frustration and near-impotence, you wait. The minutes drag into hours, the hours seem like days, and a day is forever.

In this story I have attempted to tell of this strain in the terms of the men who stand and wait throughout this seeming eternity. Perhaps it will serve to show what breed of men it takes to set a record and the price they pay for it. Twelve hours can go by like a flash. Twelve hours can also be an eternity. It all depends on your point of view. If your name is Alec Hounslow and you're watching a stubby little bronze-painted car, heavy for its 57 cubic inches of displacement, buzz full bore around a 10-mile circle, those 12 hours can seem like forever.

If your name is Alec Hounslow, you have spent months putting horses, 70-odd of them, into the 949 cc's where only 35 lived before. If your name is Sidney Enever, you have spent months of afterhours' time on the dynamometer and slide rule, figuring out just how much Alec had to get out of that engine to push 1700 pounds of car at 135 miles an hour or better for 12 hours. And if your name is George Eyston, you have spent untold hours sorting out myriad small and large details, arranging transportation, making lists and seeing that those lists were filled out with material goods, arranging living accommodations, and figuring out how to make the most out of a month on a sea of salt desert halfway around the world. You've done this in order that twenty-two crates and upwards of thirty people would all arrive at this desolate, sun-drenched spot at the proper time, so that Alec's engine could push Sidney's car faster (officially) than it, or anybody else's similar car, had ever gone before over that period of time.

Now that stubby little bronze car is out on the huge expanse of salt and one man, or rather one of three you (George Eyston) have selected, is doing his level best to make the car do what you have planned it should do. Dazzled by a brilliant sun glistening on white salt, deafened by a thousand different mechanical noises, and bereft of all sense of speed because of the lack of anything to judge by, one man is trying to maintain the exact average speed you've told him to set. His job isn't easy either. That 10-mile circle is as accurate and as even as men could make it, but it varies. Here it is as hard and smooth as new concrete but elsewhere along that 10 miles of sheer white nothing, it is bumpy, or windy, or wet and slippery. It isn't just a matter of poking a throttle until the tachometer reads 6000 rpm and holding it there. Nor is it just a matter of cranking a few degrees right lock on the steering wheel and holding. Those bumps and slippery spots and gusts of wind all must be taken into account. Engine speed and steering lock must be varied time and again during

"Thumbs up" to Tom Wisdom from Alec Hounslow as Tommy takes the 100-mile record. Bonneville, September, 1959.

each 10-mile circuit; yet, if the car is going to do what it is supposed to, the *average* speed must remain the same. Each lap must be made at some fraction between 4 minutes, 16 seconds and 4 minutes, 17 seconds—no faster, no slower. And it has to be done hour after hour for a full half a day, mile after mile—a distance equivalent to half the breadth of the United States.

If your name is Hounslow, Enever, or Eyston you know all this because you've seen it all before. You know that a couple of ounces of inadvertent pressure on the throttle can blow that little engine sky high or that a sudden slick spot can precipitate wheelspin with the same effect. Those bumps can cause a tire tread to separate. A gust of wind could send the car into a quick series of spins which, at the very least, would drop the average or negate the chance of a record or, at worst, wreck the car. You know that any piece of metal has its fatigue point. You know a thousand things that could happen and every one of them trudges or flashes through your mind. You know all this and so you sit and sweat.

For Eyston, Enever, and Hounslow, eternity began at dawn, September 9, 1959. It began when Tommy Wisdom, a British motoring writer and driver punched the starter button on EX 219, setting a mildly supercharged Austin Healey Sprite engine into stuttering life, dropped the car into gear and buzzed off on the first lap of the 160 trips around the big circle.

The first worry was wind. Cold and thin, it came in gusts of 4 to 10 miles an hour. At dawn the salt is damp with surface moisture. Wind plus slick salt could mean trouble, but Tommy's standing lap was 120 mph. His second was 140. His third lap was down to 135. Up went the signal board with the broad arrow pointing upward: "faster." The next lap was 139 and succeeding laps were between 140 and 138. The first national record fell in under five laps at 50 kilometers. In rapid succession came the 50-mile, 75-mile, 100-kilometer, 100-mile, and 200-kilometer records. Then came the first big one, the international 200-mile mark at 138.15 mph. Within the first 3 hours, twelve national records had dropped.

Following his instructions, Tommy cut the switch and went into neutral at the 9-mile mark and coasted for the pits. He came in hot, coasting at over 100 as he passed the timing lights. Moving fast, lacking any means of knowing his speed except that he was moving too fast, he shot 100 feet past the pit on the outside. Shoved back by the willing crew, he hopped out. Gus Ehrman was up next.

"Mind the wet spot at Post One—and it's still bumpy at Three," Tommy had time to shout before Hounslow buttoned Gus into the already refueled car.

Ehrman poked the button and was off. The pit stop was

so quick that the average had dropped only a mile an hour, to 138.85, the speed at which the national and international 500-kilometer marks fell, on Ehrman's standing lap. His 120-mph standing lap cut the average still further, but only to 137.72 at the national and international 500-mile mark.

Now began the agony of waiting. The first major mark sought after was the 6-hour point, which stood at 132.13. One minor mistake could cost the time that would drop the average by 5 mph. Gus *had* to stay in the car and the car *had* to stay on the course. The 3-hour record had fallen to Wisdom on his next-to-last lap. The 1000-km mark had also fallen, but the main mark had to wait until Gus finished his stint. Finally, the sixth hour came.

Another mark passed—this time the 200-mile mark. Hounslow writes the good news on blackboard flashing at Wisdom.

"Give him two more, then bring him in," Enever told Hounslow. Alec, the third fingernail on his right hand between his teeth, nodded. The other two nails were down to the quick. Captain Eyston brought back the official word: 139.09 mph was the pace they had to keep for the next 6 hours.

Gus came in, mindful of Tommy's overshoot, bringing it down in gear and clearing it at the last moment with a blast at the throttle that made Hounslow wince.

Ed Leavens, of Canada, was up next for what was, at least from the drivers' point of view, the roughest shift of all. By this time it was noon—past noon—and a merciless sun shone down from a cloudless sky. The glare was blinding, the air was hot with an ambient temperature of over 85 degrees. And, finally, there was little glory to be gained. Only one record could fall in the next 3 hours, and that one fairly early. The rest of the time was steady grind, aiming for the average. The 1,000-mile mark fell soon enough at 138.55. Leavens continued to turn the circle at a desperately boring 140 mph, give or take a fraction, working toward the setup that would assure the 12-hour record, come what may.

At about this point, if you're Captain George Eyston, you sit in the timer's shed with an outward calm born of years of record setting. But you keep an eye on the clock and a sensitive ear cocked for engine sounds or the ringing of the phone from an observer's post, a call that can only signal trouble.

If you're Sidney Enever, you pace the pit area incessantly, occasionally stopping by the cook shack, but mainly intent on sight and sound of the car. You stand in the pit shed and fidget.

If you're Alec Hounslow, you've started working on the first nail of the left hand. You wonder audibly if the engine still has that crisp, clear note it had at dawn. Is it your imagination, or has that sharp, biting rasp turned a bit feathery?

As the hours go by all you can do is wait—wait for the time when your driver must pull in for fuel and relief.

If you're any one of the thirty-odd people gathered in the pit area, you feel the tension building.

Someone says, "That's an awful little engine to lug all that weight that fast." You just look at him and he shuts up. He's right, of course, but you just don't say it. Not out loud.

By now the sun is beginning to slant in from the west. Shadows grow, black against the glaring salt. The air seems hotter than it is, and the wind has dropped to near zero.

Now it's 3:45, time to bring Leavens in. Wisdom buckles on his crash hat. The crew gathers. Any action will be a relief.

Ed cuts it clean and far out, coasting silently in; the only sound is the crunch of tires, pressurized with nitrogen to 50 pounds, crushing the hard salt. Twenty-five gallons of fuel quickly flow into the tank; a quart of oil glunks into the sump. Down with the lid and cockpit cover and Wisdom is out once more, this time for the final 2½ hours that, if all goes well, will boost the 12-hour Class G record by 20 miles an hour.

The atmosphere now is slightly reminiscent of a bomber base sweating out a mission. There's nothing to do but wait. It's all up to Tommy and the car.

The minutes trudge by on leaden feet, slogging slowly into the eleventh and final hour. The eleventh hour! You can't help it—you recall all the things that killed victory in all the races you remember. If you're Eyston, Enever, or Hounslow, you remember the last half of the last lap of a record run with this same car when a tire tread let go, snatching certain victory away. You remember Stirling Moss at Monte Carlo in 1959, with the race all tucked away and stroking it, when the gearbox packed up in that last hour. These and hundreds more near-misses stretching into racing history all march through your head. It doesn't help. Not a bit.

Then the phone jangles.

The round little man who is the official pit observer answers. He, who alone among those in the pit seemed unconcerned before, literally yanks the instrument off its mounts. A big grin lights his face.

"You're in," he says, hanging the horn back up on the wall. "He can push it in now and you've still got the record. If he stopped now and pushed, he'd still have a 122 average."

Tension drops for an instant.

Fine, you're in. But you didn't come out here to win by a fluke. The record is in; it's on the books, but Tommy doesn't know it and to hell with technicalities.

So you sweat some more. The last half hour rolls around. Then, agonizingly, the last few minutes.

Whoom go the ten walls and Tommy is on the last lap. The 12-hour record is now 138.7 mph average.

Eternity ended at 6:20 P.M., September 9, 1959.

But not anxiety. EX 219 still had more to do.

There was still a 1-hour run on the circle to be done. All the 1-hour standing start records were held by Lotus and all were 140 mph or better, except the 1-hour record itself, which stood at 137.26.

All this was to be done with a second engine, basically the same as the 12-hour machine, but a little more fierce. A little richer running, burning a rather nasty blend of fuel and twisting a little tighter—that was the difference. This time 99 horses lived where 35 belonged.

And it had to be stuffed into EX 219, which meant virtual dismantling and rebuilding in *one* night. So, it was ordered and so it was done. It was done by a crew of the hardest-working mechanics one could ask to see, and it was done by morning.

At noon, all hands assembled on the salt. Hounslow fired up the car and started out on a warm-up run, leaving in his wake the fragrant aroma of nitrobenzene. In a few minutes he was back in the pit shed. The "hard" racing plugs were installed and Gus Ehrman, who was to make the hour-long run, got in for a full-bore check ride. No sweat here—just take it around and see what she'll do.

The little engine fired up with an ear-cracking blast, and Gus shot out of the shed, tires churning up a spray of salt. Then it happened.

The sound of the engine rose sharply, then fell off. Then it rose sharply again, much too quickly for normally expected acceleration. Gus turned the car around and headed back. He pulled in and lifted the canopy.

"It's the clutch," he said. "It won't hold anything over 4,000 revs."

Buttoned snugly into the tight shell, the clutch and its linkage could not be seen—only felt by groping fingers. This one Hounslow worked on himself. There was only one thing to do. By feel and touch alone, he must undo the linkage and try the car out in one gear. For an hour busy, skilled fingers

groped until the slave cylinder was disconnected from the linkage and the clutch plates were as free to hold as they would
ever be. Hounslow jumped in the car and twenty eager pair
of hands pushed him off in third gear. The sputtering turned
into a mutter, then to a rumble which rose to a clear buzz,
as the car disappeared around the circle. All the way around
this time.

Soon he was back. "Looks like linkage all right—try it in
top gear, Gus."

Again a score of hands pushed hard and fast. Again the
car muttered off into the glare. And again it made the distance.

"All right, now try three fast ones," Ehrman was told
when he came around. Again he set off, and when he came by
he was storming, the car kicking up a light spray of salt the
way only a car going 150 or more can do. The next lap was
timed and the time was just over 4 minutes for 151 mph. It
looked good until Gus pulled the car in at the end of the
third lap.

"It's still no good," he said. "It comes undone at just
over 6,000."

What to do? If you are Hounslow or Enever, you make
a tough decision. You pack up and go back to town for another
all-night session. And this time you decide to test. You don't
have any test equipment, but you must test anyway. You
scrounge around town until you find a 100-pound spring balance, the kind they used to weigh ice with. Then you weld a
2-foot bar onto a splined socket that just fits the output shaft
of the gearbox. You do this because you know that the engine
puts out 86 lbs/ft of torque at 5800 rpm. You know that if
you hooked the spring balance on the bar exactly 2 feet from
the socket end, and if the socket end was attached to the main-
shaft, you should be able to pull at least 50 pounds on the
scale without making the shaft turn. If it turns, then, the
clutch is no good. If it doesn't you're in business. Meanwhile,
your mechanics undo the work they did the night before. And
by 11 that night they had the engine on the floor.

Left to right: Ed Leavens, Tom Wisdom and Captain Eyston wait for Gus Ehrman and listen for the sound of the car. Strain begins to show.

Four mechanics held the engine. Enever held the crank nose and Hounslow applied the scale and bar. It held at 40 on the scale—80 lbs/ft. At 45, it began to move, and at 50 it slipped easily. It just wouldn't hold the torque. Period.

Now there was only one thing to do—remove the clutch from the engine that had just gone full bore for 12 full hours, clean it up, and try it with the bar and scale. Just to be sure, the flywheel and motor plate were removed from the 12-hour engine and installed on the sprint mill.

After this work was completed the bar was applied again, while willing hands held the engine. Hounslow heaved. The scale moved up—40, 45, 50, 60, 70, 80 pounds—and still the clutch held. It was the equivalent of 160 lbs/ft of torque, and 125 to 130 would do the trick.

On through the night they worked, and at 9 in the morning the job was done. Once more on the salt, Gus took off. Within a lap he was crackling along at 153 mph and giving the high sign to the pit as he passed. Then he came in. His only complaint was that things seemed slicker than usual, a natural reaction since the car was now wearing Dunlop R5 tires that had been buffed down until only 2 millimeters of tread were left. These replaced the normal R5's worn earlier. The reason for this buffing, of course, was to lighten the tread to make absolutely sure that it wouldn't separate from the carcass. But the tires *were* slippery.

The car was pushed back behind the timing lights and the engine lighted off. The flag fell; Gus was off in a smooth, clear rush. It was a good start—his standing lap was a nice healthy 134 mph. His second was 153 and his third was 152.5. The fourth lap took longer. Lots longer.

Captain Eyston brought the word. Gus had spun out, doing seven loops before pulling out of it. Morning dampness, slick salt, and smooth tires had made 153 mph a shade too fast.

If you are Sid Enever or Alec Hounslow or Captain Eyston, what do you do now? The average is down but is it down enough to pack it all up and start over? There is only one thing to do—sit tight and watch the clock to see if the average is above the record. It is, so you sit and wait while the minutes turn into the seeming hours they were on the long previous run. You sit and hold your breath for long moments at a time while your driver holds the car to what must be the barest ragged edge of adhesion. The minutes drag by, and eventually all the intermediate marks have fallen except the 50-mile mark, missed because of that horrendous spin. The 1-hour mark should be in the bag at something around 146, but anything can happen and it does.

Another spin, this time a vicious whip to the inside of the circle. Gus re-enters the circle half a mile down the course, but the damage is done. It isn't time that's lost on this one—the average is still up above 145, some 7 mph above the existing record. The previous records are still held, but you're dead for the one hour. Disqualified for leaving the course toward the inside and not re-entering it at the point it was left—an inadvertent short cut. It's heartbreaking, but there's only one thing to do. You pat Gus on the back and break the news—he's got to do it again.

This time the car was equipped with the regular un-buffed R5's for a better bite at the salt. It was moved back to the line for a new chance—the third try for 1 seemingly measly hour when 12 had gone off without a hitch 2 days before. The flag fell and Gus was off—again.

And this time, if you're Eyston, or Enever, or Hounslow, or any other man on the team, you really sweat. So far on this one Fate has dealt you every dirty hand in the book, and you know very well there are still a hundred things that can black-ball you once again. So, if you're Hounslow, you gnaw at what nails are left from the other day. If you're Enever, you pace and fidget. If you are the tall, gracious, graying man named Eyston, you sit and stare at the timer. And, if you are Gus Ehrman, you bore 'round and 'round, bending every effort to stay on the course and maintain just the 147 mph you've been told to make. With the new tires it feels much more secure, especially since it is now past noon and the hungry sun has sucked up much of the moisture that plagued you earlier. It's easy to exceed the limit and unconsciously you do so. You and all your teammates also know that this is not the 12-hour engine. It's a nitrated, over-stressed, 99-horsepower mite that was built to make one run for the hour and a sprint up and down the straight. Will it last the distance after all the trials and false starts it has been through?

It would and it did. Without a single hitch and without

missing a beat, it picked off the hour record and five intermediate marks, raising them by 3 to 6 mph each.

John Thornely, General Manager of MG and head of
the company that built EX 219, put it best: "We're all tidy
now," he said.

At least until some other dawn.

2. "What Gear Am I In?"
by Dennis May

It is extremely doubtful if any international motor-racing figure, with the possible exception of Archie Scott Brown, ever rose to greater eminence under worse physical handicaps than Lt. Col. A. T. G. Gardner. It is also extremely doubtful if there ever was such an archetype of a Briton in any such venture or a more atypical racing man. Equipped with the peculiar cold, raw, physical and mental courage that led many of Britain's young aristocracy to heroic death against the enemy in two World Wars, Gardner was a genius in the cockpit of a record car. But from a mechanical standpoint, he was a near-moron out of it. The mechanics of a racing car were a total mystery to the man who led Britain's record men and remained the leader for the duration of his racing life. Despite such seeming paradox, this tortured, aristocratic man very likely set more speed records than any one person before or since.

A man doesn't have to be an authority on cooperage and hydrodynamics to be pushed over Niagara Falls in a barrel; and the career of Arthur Thomas Goldie Gardner is living proof that ignorance of automotive technicalities is no bar to the record-breakers hall of fame.

As the first driver to reach 200 miles per hour in the 1100- and 1500-cc categories, also the first to pass the 150-mph mark on 750 and 500 cc, he was the central figure in exploits of a technical merit at least equal to the land-speed record itself. Yet among his entourage of brains there wasn't one who'd have let him check his own tire pressures. "The Colonel" had the courage of thirty-seven Gunga Dins—and he did what he was told. It was enough.

25

It was enough except on occasions when, through some oversight, the self-evident was not explained to Goldie. Then anything could happen. One such time was Wednesday, November 9, 1938, memorable as the date of the first records he ever made with EX 135, his MG streamliner. He had raced through the mile and kilometer traps on the Frankfurt-Darmstadt autobahn at a decimal below 180 mph average. Past the end of the timed stretch, at a point where the car's speed would still be up around 170, an MG engineer had established a one-person observatory on the sidelines. At Gardner's approach the MG man took a couple of paces out on to the pavement and waved Goldie the top 'o the morning. EX 135 had back-wheel brakes only, and these were totally devoid of ventilation. But, since nobody had thought to tell the Colonel that you don't hit such brakes at 170, he hit them. By a remarkable combination of luck and legerdemain, he brought the streamliner to a standstill without doing a loop . . . just. Always the personification of *phlegme Brittanique,* Gardner had fully recovered his composure by the time the anxious technician came panting up.

"Tell me," he said, "what gear am I in?"

This suicidal act of braking, and the quaint question that followed it, might have been credible in a novice. But Goldie had been driving cars of all types and nationalities for over two decades and racing fourteen years. Before acquiring EX 135 in 1938, he was already the holder of the 1100-cc lap record for Brooklands track at better than 124 mph, and an earlier autobahnstorming trip with his first Magnette, an offset-bodied monoposto, had given him the world's fastest Class G speed in 1937.

Many years later, in a place far removed from Frankfort-am-Main, the Colonel gave his aides the last of many reminders that he was no Uhlenhaut. After two turns of a 10-mile circle on the Bonneville Salt Flats, in quest of Class E records in '52, he pulled out and worriedly reported that the oil thermometer

During his final series of record attempts, Gardner, in a typical pose, rests his shattered leg.

hand was now on its second lap of the dial. Disproof of this novel contention did not defeat the brain of Sydney Enever, Chief Engineer of MG, whose technical skill had contributed more than any other man's to EX 135's long and varied list of record kills.

With the close of this Bonneville chapter, Lt. Col. A.T.G. Gardner, O.B.E., M.C., took his weight off the MG's canted-back hammock seat for the last time. Ill health forced him to abandon plans for another Utah expedition in 1953; thus ended the man-and-machine partnership that had lasted 9 peacetime years, bridged a world war, and set fastest-ever marks in 60 per cent of the recognized international classes, from 350 cc to 2 liters.

Ironically, although the 1952 edition of EX 135, powered by a blown TD engine of basically stock pushrod type, took American national records at over the 200 mark, Gardner was cheated by a tantalizingly narrow margin of his real target; this was to beat his own 13-year-old Class F marks—203.5 and 203.2 mph for the mile and kilometer set in '39 with six cylinders and a single overhead camshaft under the carapace.

"A gentleman to the ferrule of his walkingstick" was the most apt description of Gardner I ever heard. The allusion to the stick was more than incidental. This accessory, which he had the habit of hanging by its crook from one of his jacket pockets when standing easy, was the symbol of a physical handicap that dogged him with varying degrees of rigor for nearly 40 years. Every race he drove, every record he attacked, had its accompaniment of unpleasant sensation ranging from nagging discomfort to acute pain. I was with him on many races and record sorties, at home in Britain and abroad in Belgium, France, and the United States, and I never heard him utter more than an undertoned grunt of complaint.

With a crippled right leg and hip like his, lesser men would have never entered the cockpit of a racing car; Goldie, on the contrary, made his handicap the reason for getting *into* this department of speedwork. When his injuries robbed him of the freedom of movement demanded by road racing, he just switched to a branch of the business in which he'd only need agility for crawling out from under in event of wrecks.

He received the original damage in a flying accident while on home leave from France in 1917. Following a 2-year layup in a hospital and twenty operations, he was ruled unfit for service and discharged from the army. A man's fitness for automobile racing, however, is naturally his own affair, and medical opinion was, therefore, not invited when Major A.T.G. Gardner made his Brooklands debut in the summer of 1924, driving the species of Austin Seven known as a Gordon England Special. How, with his six feet, three inches of stature and a right knee devoid of a knee-action, he ever shoehorned himself into the little car remains a mystery. And the immediate successors to the G.E. Special, a Salmson, an Amilcar and a Montlhéry Midget MG, weren't very much roomier.

Not content with the interim job they'd made of smashing up his leg in '17, Goldie's gremlins tailed him to the Ards circuit, Northern Ireland, in 1932, and tried again in the Tourist Trophy race. Crowded off onto a grassgrown shoulder while maneuvering to pass a slower driver on a fast run, he hit a transverse gulley with his front wheels. The Midget went end over end three times. At the second inverted landing it came down on top of him, inflicting a compound fracture of the right leg, close above the knee, and other injuries of a lesser order. His helmet split open like a nutshell under the impact but, nevertheless, saved his life.

Complications set in, including septicemia, and for weeks it was uncertain whether amputation would be necessary. Finally, the surgeons managed to conjure some semblance of life back into the limb and, after 4 month in the hospital, Gardner returned home, with both legs intact. On this point, incidentally, some British newspapermen took a lot of convincing; right up to the time of his first 200-mph bursts in

1939, the nontechnical press regularly referred to Goldie as "The One-Legged Major," or "The One-Legged Speed Ace."

The appellation "Major" was accurate at that date. It wasn't until his World War II service with the Royal Artillery that Gardner rose to the rank of Lieutenant Colonel. As such, of course, he wasn't and isn't officially entitled to be addressed as Colonel, but with his rather naive regard for the grandiose he was not the man to disown this extra-military promotion. When he was in Italy in 1946, shooting at 750-cc records, an Italian factotum attached to his equipe elevated him to Sir Colonel Gardner, then to Mr. General Gardner. It is not on record that Goldie corrected him.

To get a proper perspective on the guts of the man, all of his speed exploits between 1924 and 1952 have to be viewed in the light of his disability. The injuries he took at Ards, needless to say, did nothing to improve his already-weak leg. From then on, the pain spasms became progressively worse and more frequent, usually coming at the least convenient times. Nevertheless, except for finally quitting speedwork on doctors' orders when he finally submitted to doctors' orders and quit in 1953—through a health deterioration unconnected with his leg—he never canceled or even postponed a record bid because of his handicap.

Short as he was on engineering knowledge, Goldie was far from lacking imagination; he knew well enough that if EX 135 ever flew off the handle at upwards of 3 miles a minute, his chances of wriggling out of the wreckage were reduced to practically zero due to the tight fit imposed by his above-average height and his lack of elasticity. Once in the cockpit, leaning back in his hammock at the 40-degree angle dictated by frontal-area rationing and with the oblong-shaped steering wheel snapped into place athwart his stomach, he was surely *in*.

Moreover, even if it never came to the point of having to jettison the wheel for a breakout—and it didn't—it wasn't difficult to imagine circumstances where the MG's limited helm movement could render the driver practically helpless. Lock-to-lock range, circumscribed by the side sections of the nose fairing, was only 18 degrees; if, for any reason, the car went into a spin, or in the likelier event of an unexpected gust of wind nudging it off course to any appreciable extent, the Colonel knew he would be in serious trouble.

The only time that either of these things happened, as good luck would have it, was in the one records area on his list where it could happen without danger—Bonneville. This was during his final foray in 1952, and followed soon after the oil-temperature hallucination recalled earlier. Operating EX 135 with the larger of the interchangeable engines that were taken to the Flats that year—a 2-liter Wolseley job, type VC22— Goldie started chasing his tail at 155 mph on slick salt.

Again, in 1948 on the Jabbeke Highway in Belgium, when Jaguar lent a 2 liter XK 100 engine for use in EX 135, there were delicious excitements. On one of the two runs that gave Goldie an over-all average of 176.6 mph for the flying kilometer, the right-front tire tread flew off throwing the wheel into an out-of-balance tantrum before disintegrating and falling out on to the concrete. This could have been deadly, due to the confined space inside the wheel boxes that were built into EX 135's shell to reduce pumping losses. But it wasn't.

It wasn't until after Goldie's triumphant return to his hotel in Ostend the same evening that he was told how nearly he had missed being intercepted in the middle of the trap by positively the slowest rig in Jabbeke, a donkey cart. I happened to be an eyewitness to this affair, and it frightened me stiff.

As Gardner came streaking down the road at a good 175, the donkeyman, apparently deaf but anyway oblivious, emerged from one of the few unguarded farm exits on the entire 6-mile course. Confused by the frenzied "giddaps" coming at him in three languages and from four directions, the

donkey froze in the middle of the highway. With just seconds
to spare, the whole outfit was half lifted, half dragged to the
nearest verge.

Characteristically, in the course of his many visits to the
United States, he hobnobbed with countless notables, from
Clark Gable through Pop Myers to one of the Vice Presidents
of the United States. The only surprising thing is that he
settled for the Vice President.

On the other hand, he was invariably considerate and
courteous to his mechanics and all persons dependent upon
him, and he never missed an opportunity of publicly praising
their efforts. Guts, or the lack of it, is something a race
mechanic can smell a mile away, and the men who worked
on EX 135 and her predecessors knew that Goldie had more
fight in him than a lion with a bullet wound.

I once heard a tire fitter say of him, in the vernacular of
his trade, "The old man never shows his breaker strip." The
speaker knew that Goldie, like any person of imagination,
had a breaker strip to show, and there were times when long
and unforseen delays pending a critical record would stretch
his nerves to snapping point; but outwardly, by the habit of
self-discipline that is often observable in old soldiers, he pre-
served a flat calm—no fussing, no cussing, no tabbing out of
half-smoked cigarettes (he always smoked a straight-grain pipe,
anyway), no poking his nose into mechanical mysteries beyond his modest ken.

As Goldie Gardner would certainly agree, only a fraction
of the credit for EX 135's attainments rightly belongs to him
—the rest is divided among Sydney Enever and R. C. Jackson
of MG, Ken Taylor and Reid Railton of the famous Thomp-
son and Taylor partnership, independent expediter Robin
Jackson, S.U. mastermind Kes Kesterson, Wally Hassan of
Jaguar, Chris Shorrock of the Shorrock blower team, and
many who remained anonymous throughout. Yet, Goldie and
the steamliner were so inseparably associated that no profile

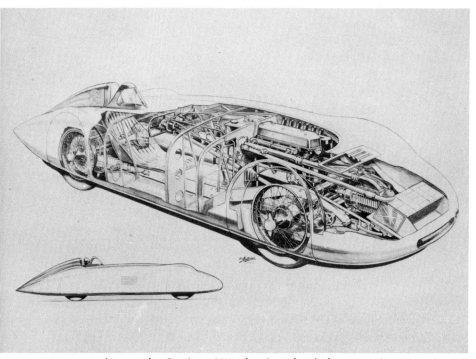

Cutaway view of the Gardner MG showing chassis layout and super-charged K-3 Magnette MG engine. Car later had a completely enclosed cockpit.

of him would stand scrutiny unless it included a catalog of his car's principal successes. Arranged in descending order of displacements, it looks like this:

Class E, 1500 to 2000 cc: First car to exceed 150 mph, powered by Jaguar XK100 motor. This was the only class in which Gardner went outside the Nuffield Group for an engine. EX 135 hoisted the kilometer mark, previously held by a Franco-U.S. Derby-Miller, by over 30 mph.

Class F, 1100 to 1500 cc: First car to beat 220 mph, 300 kph, and 3 miles per minute.

Class G, 750 to 1100 cc: Same again. Gardner's 1110-cc speeds in 1939 corresponded almost exactly to Segrave's land-speed-record figures of only 12 hours earlier. Segrave had

needed 24 cylinders, each of them 122 by 160 millimeters.
Class H, 500 to 750 cc: First to go over 150 mph.
Class I, 350 to 500 cc: First to hit 2 miles per minute, 150 and 200 kph.
Class J, up to 350 cc: First to go 2 miles per minute.

First time out, in 1938, when the second-hand EX 135 was rebuilt for Goldie Gardner's use, the engine was run at the normal K3 Magnette displacement of 1087 cc. Blown by Centric, it delivered 186 bhp and attained a best two-way speed of 186.6 mph over the kilometer.

The following year, practically unaltered, the same engine pulled a higher gear to raise its own Class G records past 200 mph, then was fractionally overbored on location to bring it inside the Class F scale. In this size, with its bores up from 57 to 59 mm, making the displacement 1105½ cc, it pushed the MG over the mile and kilometer at 203.85 and 204.28 mph, respectively. The mile speed, incidentally, added almost exactly 40 mph to a mark set by the late Frank Lockhart (Miller) 12 years earlier.

After this, his next objective was to procure a workable 750-cc six without departing from the basic K3 elements. This was done by, first, forging a short-throw crankshaft to dwarf the stroke to 56 mm and then casting a special thick-wall enabling the cylinders to be underbored at a 53-mm diameter. In the result, in spite of a perforce low nominal compression ratio of 5.1/1, the combustion of a rather high boost and an 8000-per-minute turnover produced about 131 bhp. And that was good enough for 159 mph in 1946, in the runs that inaugurated the Jabbeke Highway.

In 1935, MG anticipated a Mercedes gesture of twenty years later, turning about face from their previous policy and quitting unconditionally; so Eyston sold EX 135 for the good and sufficient reason that no racing department remained at Abingdon to breathe continued life into his striped *bolide*.

Fortunately for the subsequent history of high speed by

small British cars, Lord Nuffield and his lieutenant in charge of MG, the late Cecil Kimber, were persuaded to relent to the extent of preparing a full streamliner for Class G records. The man who made them change their minds was Arthur Thomas Goldie Gardner, himself.

Because the Abingdon stock-in-trade did not include the makings of a suitable car, there was no option but to seek out the man who had bought Eyston's super-annuated EX 135, buy it back, and rebuild it. This they did, and the veteran of the Mannin Beg, the British 500, and the hour record got a third lease on life in a suit of aerodynamic armor that was to set a fashion in streamliners for two decades to come.

Remarkably enough, like most of the amateur copies that were afterwards made of it in at least two continents, this body never saw the inside of a wind tunnel. Like all the creations of Reid A. Railton, it looked right and it was right. And this was quite fitting. Gardner wouldn't have known a laminar flow shape if it came up and pinched his leg. All he wanted was a car that would carry him to as many records as he could find the time to make. Railton provided it and that's all Gardner cared about. He was that kind of a man.

3. Big Car—Big Speed
by Martyn Denis

Dusk had fallen on the vast, barren, white Bonneville salt flats; the twilight was rather gloomy after the almost-unbearable brilliance of the day. Out of the distance came a sharp buzzing that grew and grew until it became a painful shriek. Then, although the volume continued to increase, the pitch fell off to a roar and then to a crackling burble. A sudden burst, and then stillness, broken only by the sound of rock-hard tires crunching the salt, preceded the tiny green teardrop-shaped car. A tall, bespectacled, scholarly looking man walked over to congratulate the driver. For the first time, Captain George Eyston (pronounced *Ee*ston) was on the salt flats on an excursion in which he did not drive. The occasion was the record-smashing 245-1-mph run by Stirling Moss in the latest MG streamliner, EX 181.

Moss is among the top ten of today's drivers. But more than impeccable skill and a good right foot are needed to break records. It's the team that counts and MG had wisely picked Britain's foremost living record man as team captain. Ironically, the car they used was perhaps the smallest 200-plus mph car ever, and throughout the year Captain George Eyston had steadfastly maintained one major belief—that for big speed one needed a big car. He lived by the belief, too. Each succeeding increase in speed was made in a successively larger car, his culminating 350-plus being turned in the city-bus-proportioned *Thunderbolt,* on record as the biggest racing car of all time.

People who design cars for the land-speed record generally have too much sense or not enough courage to drive them themselves, but there have been exceptions. One such is Captain George Eyston. Since the death of John Cobb in 1952, Eyston has been the world's fastest, living motorist. Odd as it seems in a day and age of medium-displacement sports cars with 200 mph on the tips of their tongues, only three drivers have ever beaten the triple century. Two of them, Campbell and Cobb, and dead. The third, sexagenarian George Edward Thomas Eyston, is not only alive but also a summit figure in the auto-sport worlds of two continents, equally active and honored on both sides of the Atlantic.

Eyston personally evolved the over-all designs of his cars, in 1937, these took 3-D form as *Thunderbolt,* the all-time biggest, heaviest, and most powerful automobile—30 feet long, 7 tons in weight, and harnessing 5000 horsepower from two Rolls Royce airplane engines aggregating over 73 litres. Nobody but George ever drove *Thunderbolt,* even on the warm-up runs. Three times, once in 1937 and twice the following year, the big bairn arrowed over the salt at the fastest land speed on record, first 312 mph, then 345.5, finally 357.5. Although Cobb's Railton officially was the first to exceed 350, this honor would likely have been Eyston's if the timing apparatus hadn't nodded off during the second of two runs he made on August 24, 1938. The first gave 347.16. Going back, the rev-counters showed *Thunderbolt* to be traveling appreciably faster—354 mph, Eyston estimated—but the electric eye never gave a wink. Expert diagnosis was that reflection of the sun's rays off the car's polished aluminum flanks was to blame for the eye's inaccuracy. Eyston subsequently took the timekeepers' advice and had the offending surfaces painted matte black, but before he could again hit his August-24 form, Cobb had made a round-trip average of 350.2.

Steered as it was through two interconnected pairs of front wheels, *Thunderbolt* was sometimes facetiously referred to

as "Eyston's four-in-hand." Coincidentally, his earliest experience in relatively fast travel on wheels had been at the reins
of a veritable four-in-hand. During George's boyhood, his
father had been famous for miles around the 400-year-old an-
cestral seat of the Eystons at East Hendred, Berkshire, as an
amateur coachman. In unbending moods Eyston *père* would
shift over on the box and give young George the whip hand
for spells. By further coincidence, a favorite objective of these
excursions was the ancient Red Lion Inn at Abingdon, just
down the road from the site of the future MG factory, from
which would roll, almost a quarter of a century later, the
Eyston-designed Magic Midget and Magic Magnette record
cars.

When *Thunderbolt* finally perished by fire at Wellington,
New Zealand, during an exhibition tour, nobody could say
she didn't have it coming. Cars, like men, "owe God a death,"
and the *Thunderbolt*-Eyston partnership made several feints
at settling the debt. Perhaps their narrowest and luckiest
escape was one that to my knowledge has never been reported
up to this writing. Apart from the driver himself, there were
no eyewitnesses to the affair.

It happened on the salt in 1938, during *in camera* trials
following the 357.5-mph record. Eyston and his technicians
had reason to believe, as a result of on-the-spot moods and
George's improving familiarity with the brute, that the car
was already capable of considerably higher speeds than those
officially clocked. These private tests, conducted after the
departure of the timekeepers and other hitherto-interested
parties, were for the purpose of confirming paper calculations
with a view to new attempts in the future. According to Bert
Denly, who was first on the scene after the lame monster
had reeled and gyrated to a lopsided halt, *Thuderbolt* was
making close to 400 mph when the anchorage of one of the
rear suspension wishbones broke, clenching the wheel against
the chassis girder and locking it solid.

Eyston on salt during his last record attempt with the Thunderbolt. Note the size of the huge streamliner compared with 1937 Oldsmobile.

Denly's recollection of Eyston's reaction is that "he didn't say much." In crises, of which he has had his fair share in his years of speed on land and water, Eyston never has said much.

Although it was his nature to make light—or more exactly, to refrain from making anything—of his miraculous deliverances, George didn't intend to leave Bonneville on a bier if he could help it. G.E.T. Eyston's role was not to be that of a dead hero. Thus, when *Thunderbolt's* cockpit was sealed right in under a transparent dome as part of a general aerodynamic improvements program in the winter of 1937-38, he decided that in future he would always use a respirator. He had worn one (surmounting his famous asbestos suit) while breaking records on tight-fitting Midgets at Montlhéry years earlier, so he was inured to humorists' allusions to bagpipes. At Bonneville, as it developed, the gas mask undoubtedly saved his life. Chassis modifications for 1938 had included a change over to servo operation for *Thunderbolt's* disc brakes (there were windjammer panels behind the cockpit as well). The first time on, at around 260 mph, the servo did a square job on pedal-push multiplication and burned the linings to powder in half a mile. The brakes, which were located approximately alongside Eyston's shins, burped the resulting smoke and fumes directly into the cockpit through the pedal slots. Completely blinded, but at least able to breathe, George steered by guess for interminable seconds. *Thunderbolt* veered right, into the clear. If it had gone the other way, it probably would have smashed into one of its own replenishment depots, where a score of mechanics stood frozen to their footprints in fear for the Captain's life.

The power output I have quoted for this car, 5000 bhp, was the final figure, reached in 1938 after a great deal of work on the engines and their appurtenances. The enormous forward-facing airscoops, for instance, jutting from the deck behind the cockpit, were still further increased in size, and thereby enabled 73 litres of engine to swallow 200,000 litres of air per minute at maximum power.

Various important drag-defeating measures were adopted, too, in addition to the sealing in of the cockpit already mentioned. The big tail fin was removed and so was the radiator, the latter's air-intake aperture being stoppered off with a sort of sheet-metal goiter that must have greatly improved the car's penetrative qualities. In the short time available, however, it wasn't possible to rig up ice tanks through which the coolant could circulate (*à la Railton*), an omission that led to George's being almost boiled alive the last time he felled the L.S.R. As he afterwards wrote. "We had not reached the measured distance before the heat flow from the hot water in the nose became almost intolerable. I knew I would have to stick it out for quite a while, but each second the heat intensified, roaring up like a blast from a furnace. . . . I knew there was little margin, so that perhaps a couple of dozen joints in the water piping might spring a leak under the strain, and a mass of boiling water pour out."

In round figures, *Thunderbolt's* power-weight ratio was just about equal to that of Cobb's *Railton*, which was approximately half as powerful and half as heavy. The *Railton's* best two-way speed (prewar), 369.70 mph, was only 12 mph up on the mighty four-in-hand, the former's smaller cross section and aerodynamic shape accounting for the difference.

If Eyston had a one-track mind, so had Leonardo da Vinci. George's record cars covered an engine-displacement range of over 72 litres, from 750 Midgets to *Thunderbolt*—a kind of a record in itself. His single-engine Bonneville car, *Speed of the Wind,* was unique in its field because of its front-wheel drive; if it were still around today, which it isn't—the Luftwaffe laid an egg on it during the war—this one would still, I think, be the world's fastest pull-instead-of-push car. *Thunderbolt* was the only L.S.R. contender ever built with more than four wheels (it had six—or eight if you count double for the twins at the back). *Flying Spray,* which was actually *Speed of the Wind* fitted with a Ricardo diesel engine, was the sole British candidate for world's-fastest honors in the C.I. class; it held this record, with a kilometer speed of 159.1 mph, for many years. Also, the 24-hour mark set before World War II by Eyston's Chrysler-A.E.C. oil burner, 97.05 mph, has never yet been beaten. In the early '30s George was a jump ahead of Fred Dixon in adapting Riley sixes to take a separate carb per inlet port; he disclaims inventor's right to the idea, however, recalling that it originated on Millers in the United States.

Eyston, unlike many of the best brains in the race-and-records business, was not self-taught. He had a formal education in mechanical engineering at Cambridge university, immediately after serving with distinction in the British army throughout World War I. But nature equipped him with something that perhaps has served him better than whole libraries of books ever could: a receptive mind, a venturesome angle of attack on technical problems, and a readiness to heed and profit by the experience of others. In the company of people with even modest pretensions to engineering authority, or authority on any subject on earth for that matter, he has a characteristic way of listening absorbedly with his head tilted slightly to one side . . . and not saying much.

The f.w.d. car, which, like *Thunderbolt,* was designed in outline by George himself, served as a laboratory for several experiments in the distinctive and unconventional Eyston idiom. One of these, put on *Speed of the Wind,* rather late in its life, took the form of a big nose fin, angled at about 8 degrees to the longitudinal axis. Combined with suspension which was biased to tilt the whole car a bit off keel, dirt-track style, this "sail" enabled George and his Bonneville partners to drive hands off, that is merely by resting their hands on the wheel, while describing 10-mile circles at better than 165. Another time a start was made grafting a small auxiliary diesel onto *Flying Spray* for the sole purpose of powering a supercharger. This exercise, although technically feasible and promising, never actually went into action on the salt.

Although some of Eyston's blueprints were, to say the least, bold, he never was in danger of developing into a dreaming abstractionist. On the contrary, his feet stayed firmly on the ground. Proof of his high rating in the eyes of unimpressionable authority was given when the British government released to him the V-12 Ricardo diesel engine used in *Flying Spray*. This engine, built in unit with a gear box designed for front drive, was one of only three or four that had ever been constructed; mere money couldn't buy them. Output of these big sleeve-valvers was surprisingly low—around 300 bhp. The unblown Rolls Royce Kestrel engine used in *Speed of the Wind* gave about 100 horsepower more.

Outstanding among the many world records set at Bonneville by *Speed of the Wind* were Eyston's 159.3 mph for one hour in 1935, and the 12-hour mark he and Denly shared in '37—163.68 mph. The fact that the 1937 average for a full day was 4 mph up on the 1935 speed for a single hour is a testimony to the heat of the competition in this era, with relentless mutual pressure maintained between the Eyston and Cobb crews on the one hand and that of Ab Jenkins on the other. These relative speeds and durations also point up the virtual unburstability of the slow-revving Kestrel.

Eyston (center), gives orders to Sydney Enever (left) and Alec Hounslow (right), on occasion of Austin-Healey Sprite record run in September, 1959.

A textbook on pitwork could have been written around the Eyston camp's feats of legerdemain in Utah. For instance, Bert Denly says that 27 seconds usually sufficed for changing all wheels, refueling, and getting rolling again with the take-over driver aboard. Denly also recalls that the sensation when turning 10- or 12-mile circles at 160-plus with front-wheel drive was unlike anything else imaginable—almost as though the back wheels didn't exist and you were balancing quite effortlessly, above the single pair in front.

Pit routine was always organized and drilled by Eyston himself, who from his earliest days in the game had schooled himself in this craft and the kindred art of team management with almost priestly zeal. Latterly, of course, his skill has been periodically exercised in Utah on behalf of BMC's serial expeditions. In August, 1959, he was in charge when EX181 and EX179 toppled Class F and G records. The last time George played a driving role in record breaking was in 1954, the year he and Ken Miles co-drove EX179 at Bonneville to an average of over 120 mph for distances and times up to 2000 kilometers and 12 hours. Back then, the car was running with an unblown MG engine. George's days of record breaking are now over, he says. It isn't that his sixty-plus years are weighing unduly heavily—he just feels he shouldn't stand in the way of younger men, that's all.

The Eyston-Deny association, which was to become one of the most potent forces in record breaking, originated by pure chance. At Brooklands one day in 1930, George was doing a marathon tire testing job for Avon, driving one of his Bugattis. In mid-stint, somebody flagged him in to attend to an urgent business matter. Anxious not to break the continuity of the tests, he buttonholed Bert, who happened to be doing nothing in particular on the sidelines, and asked him to stand in. He did. Although long famous as a motorcycle racer, Denly had never driven a fast car in his life. He nevertheless gave satisfaction in the elementary chore of wearing Avons out, so Eyston gave him other part-time commissions. The following year George hired him permanently, and thereafter he stuck with The Skipper, as he invariably calls him, right up to the war. When peace returned and Eyston became a Castrol director, the first thing he did was to call Denly and put him on the Castrol payroll in their engine-testing department. He's there still, but still accompanies The Skipper to such faraway destinations as Bonneville whenever an opportunity occurs.

If anyone ever cast a slur on his boss in Denly's hearing. Bert, who stands about five feet high, would probably climb on a chair and hit him in the stomach. That is the sort of loyalty that Eyston—with his unfailing kindness, courtesy,

Eyston and inseparable companion and co-driver, Bert Denly, stand with "Speed of the Winds."

and straight dealing—inspires in people who work with him and for him. With one home in England and another on Park Avenue, George's circles of acquaintance on both sides of the Atlantic are about equally large. Tall, broad, and white-haired, and with a fast, long-striding gait, he is a familiar figure at such U. S. speed venues as Sebring, Watkins Glen, Elkhart Lake, and Turners Field, at all of which he acts as a steward when his New York sojourns happen to coincide with races.

Of all the cars Eyston ever raced, perhaps the most self opinionated was the straight-eight Panhard, a lofty, narrow single-seater somewhat resembling a grandfather's clock laid on its side. Powered by an 8-litre, sleeve-valve engine that may have been the only one of its kind ever built, the Panhard twice broke the world's hour record, among many others, in George's hands. Possessed of a titanic understeer, this car had to be dissuaded by brute force from bee-lining over the Montlhéry bankings each time around. Denly recalls that the preliminaries to tries for long-duration records on the Panhard usually included a program of physical training. The Skipper, who had rowed for Trinity College in his Cambridge days, would go sculling on the Seine. Denly, formerly an amateur boxer of some attainments, would knock hell out of a punching bag and go for marathon runs and walks. Their bouts of combat with the Panhard always resulted in a draw, though sometimes only just.

As well as breaking records with it, George drove the Panhard in Brooklands races, the most memorable being the 100-miler around the Outer Circuit which, in 1932, inaugurated the British Empire Trophy series. This resulted in practically a photo finish between the future rivals for the L.S.R., Eyston and Cobb, the latter driving the 10-litre Delage on which René Thomas had held the land record in 1924. The judges gave the decision to Cobb—by one fifth of a second. Then Eyston, claiming he'd been inadvertently balked in a wheel-to-wheel approach to the finish line, protested to the stewards and got the verdict reversed. Cobb in his turn had the matter referred to the Royal Automobile Club, who reversed the reversal and declared John the winner after all. It was typical of George's benign nature that, rather than going away and griping under his breath, he signified his satisfaction with the R.A.C. ruling by standing Cobb a little celebration dinner . . . and thus ended The Great Who Wunnit.

Two years later, after the British Empire Trophy had been made over into a synthetic road race, run on a *chicane*-bedevilled circuit at Brooklands, Eyston won, driving his Magic Magnette. This time, due to the fact that George's pit crew either hadn't kept a proper lap count or weren't sharing their intelligence with The Skipper, he was quite unaware of his position when they flagged him off at the end. It took quite a bit to convince him that he'd won. This skepticism was understandable, because he'd always had a kind of a hoodoo on him in Brooklands classics; once he was beaten into a third placement in the Two Hundred by a fifth of a second, and twice he cracked up and had to retire after leading the Five Hundred at three-quarter distance.

Eyston, sportman and man of science, is something of a poet, too, with a tendency to relieve the grind of a records campaign by rising at 3 A.M. and tramping to some preselected vantage point to watch the sunrise and listen to birdsong.

Orderly and conscientious by temperament—he is, for instance, never late for an appointment, and he does not like people who keep him waiting—he seldom took an uncalculated risk during his speed career. A possible exception was the time at Montlhéry when his Chrysler-A.E.C. diesel, fitted with a modified sedan body, broke one of its chassis side members during a 24-hour record run. The breakage occurred 6 hours from the end, and George opted to keep on going and see what happened. With the sound girder flexing like a hula dancer's backbone, the prop shaft gradually sawed its way through an adjacent crosstie. Then the body panels, unaccustomed to a stressed-skin role, started bucking into pleats. But the Chrysler never did fold up, and the schedule was adhered to, with Eyston and Denly driving in shifts. Despite all, the record duly fell.

Between about 1927 and 1954, George's personal score of world and international records, including shared bags, was almost certainly the biggest of any Briton. If his totals were outstripped by various Frenchmen—and they were—this was because Eyston, unlike these French mass producers, was interested only in *breaking* records, as distinguished from establishing ones that nobody else had hitherto bothered to established (e.g., 59 days at 58.28 mph by Marchand and friends with a Citroen sedan in 1933, a mark that presumably stands to this day).

Aside from his Utah exploits, George's association with MG produced the most colorful and technically significant chapter of his whole records career. Eyston's initiative was directly responsible for the MG company's entry into the records field. In fact, if he hadn't propositioned them when he did, in the sense he did, it's quite possible that their prewar contribution to auto sports might never have gone further than running a few slightly modified stock cars in minor Brooklands races.

The train of events, very briefly, was this. Back in 1929, Eyston conceived an ambition to acquire, build, or adapt a car that would be capable of traveling faster on 750 cc than anything that had gone before. The short records, mile and kilometer, in international Class H were currently held by a Frenchman called Ratier, with a car of his own design and construction. First, then, George took the logical step of finding out whether this Ratier could and would make him a seven-fifty to lick the Ratier. M. Ratier tried, but the deal never came off. Next Eyston was attracted by an idea propounded by Ernest Eldridge, a friend and business associate of his, for down-scaling an 1100 Riley engine for the same purpose, and hanging it in a chassis that Parry Thomas had built for one of his 1½ litre Thomas Specials. This deal also fell short of completion.

Then George happened to cross paths with Jimmy Palmes, an old Cambridge buddy of his. By a fortuitous piece of timing, Palmes was at that moment busy sleeving down an 850-cc MG Midget—his own property—to 750 cc. His plan was to use it for an attack on the Class H 24-hours record. Intrigued, Eyston accepted Palmes' invitation to join the operation; then, between them, they enlisted the enthusiatic support of Cecil Kimber, the head of MG. Gradually developed beyond recognition of its original form, and with a potent aid to poop in the form of a Powerplus blower (which George and his technical associates had designed 4 years earlier), this formerly undistinguished Midget grew up gracefully into the world-famous EX120. Among other highlights of its sensational career, EX120 was the first seven-fifty to exceed both

Eyston, in the "Magic Midget," after setting international record of 189 kilometers-per-hour at Montlhéry, December, 1932.

100 mph and 100 miles in one hour. Its immediate successor, EX127, vulgarly styled the *Magic Midget,* was also built to George's order, and with it, at Montlhéry in 1932, The Skipper set a further Class H landmark by beating 2 miles per minute for the first time. Afterwards, it was acquired by Bobby Kaulrausch, the German, in whose hands it jacked up the 750-mile record to 140.6.

Denly a truly great trackman, made Montlhéry history on EX127 by being the only driver ever to win a 200-kph lap badge on less than 2 litres. This local record still stands. As a further but unrelated example of Bert's mastery of the art of rapid ring around o' roses, on *Speed of the Wind* at Bonneville he once turned five consecutive laps of the 10-mile circle with a maximum variation of two fifths of a second; this at over 160 per. So great was the discrepancy in size between Eyston and Denly that, when he took over the big front-drive from his chief during stage stops, Bert always had to have the Skipper-size seat removed and a special uplift affair substituted.

Although automobile history has Eyston typed as a records man, his circuit race activities and successes were by no
means paltry. In the mid-to-late '20s, for example, he won the
Boulogne GP des Voitures Légeres and the Grand Prix of La
Baule, driving various Bugattis. Alfa Romeo's concessionaires
in Britain picked him to handle their stuff in such classics as
the TT, the Irish GP, and the Brooklands Double Twelve,
and in 1929 he shared second placement with the then-famous
Boris Ivanowski in the Belgian 24-hour race at Spa. As we saw
earlier, he won the British Empire Trophy at Brooklands on
his own *Magic Magnette,* which afterwards formed the nucleus
of Goldie Gardner's 200-mph streamliner, EX135. In 1933, at
Montlhéry, George finished third on a 2.3 Alfa in the French
Grand Prix, a month or two after winning his Mille Miglia
class for MG in partnership with Count John. Lurani. The
Eyston-Lurani Magnette formed one third of an Abingdon
task force that copped the Mille Miglia team prize; Earl Howe,
who was another of the MG team members on this occasion,
had rather astutely entered his own blown Merc independently (a fellow named Penn-Hughes drove it) and loaded it to
the lid with Magnette parts in case of emergencies en route.
On paper, Penn-Hughes was in the act to race, but *de facto*
his job was to nursemaid the Magneticians. As it turned out
they didn't have any need for his wares, Eyston for his part
having learned during training, by the traditional M.M.
process of driving through railroad crossing gates when they
were closed, that it's worth waiting until somebody opens
them.

Unlike Segrave, Campbell, and Cobb, The Skipper never
reached for the water-speed crown as well as the L.S.R. He
has always had a toe in the other element, however, either on
the technical, sporting, or commercial levels. In his youth he
served an apprenticeship with Britain's biggest marine pro-
peller makers; in the early '20s he quit car speedwork for a

couple of years and raced hydroplanes instead; and he is currently a director of John I. Thorneycroft, Ltd., the international marine engineers, whose weightier occupations include repair work and refits for the *Queens*.

It was a famous American racing driver who unwittingly first infected the young marine apprentice with the itch that led him, by a long and adventurous road, to Utah and the land-speed record; in view of the part that Americans and the United States scene were to play in his subsequent fortunes, this was somehow prophetic. In 1921, Eyston went to Le Mans to spend a vacation with friends and to brush up on his French. Ranging the Sarthe countryside one day, his contemplation of nature's glories was interrupted by the sight and sound of a car approaching along a little-frequented stretch of die-straight road. It was a sight and sound that, even in George's mind, gave nature and her glories some stiff competition. From a blue-chinned mechanic, waiting at the roadside with tools and equipment, he learned that the goggled demigod crouching over the wheel of this flying projectile was Ralph de Palma, doing tests on his Ballot for the imminent French *Grand Prix*.

Eyston, as he hobbled back to Le Mans in his old 2-cylinder GN, was a thoughtful fellow. Less than 2 years later, the seed de Palma had unknowingly sown was bearing fruit. First, with Brooklands neither sitting up nor taking the slightest notice, George drove a prewar *Coupe de l'Auto* Sunbeam there. Then a 4½-litre Vauxhall. Then an ex-Zborowski GP Aston Martin. After that, the Bugs and the Alfas and an OM and a thing called a Halford. G. E. T. Eyston was on his way!

4. The Stutz That Wasn't
by Griffith Borgeson

It happened very fast, faster in fact than even the camera could follow. The little car, looking more like a white, wingless airplane than an automobile, was merely a white streak against the blue Atlantic. Suddenly, horribly, it turned itself into a ball of metal and careened down the beach at nearly 200 miles and hour, finally coming to rest at the water's edge. It had been the world's most advanced automobile and it carried with it the near-illiterate genius who was credited with being the world's most advanced automotive thinker.

In his short span of years, Frank Lockhart was so busy building better machinery that he barely took the time to learn to write his own language. From childhood, Frank lived for one thing alone—speed and the ways of attaining it. Equipped with inborn and consummate driving skill, he had something else, too—an absolute and utter genius for improving the work of other men. For Frank, not even the brilliance of Harry Miller, America's foremost racing-car designer, was good enough. It was Lockhart who discovered the method of heat treating the overly brittle and fragile valves of the Miller engine, and it was Lockhart who, with Leon Duray, thought of the supercharger intercooler that made the supercharger practical and reliable.

The little white car that ended his life was to have been the culmination—the pinnacle—of a brilliant career. It was to have provided the fame and money that would allow that career to blossom unhampered. But it didn't —it merely ended a man's life on the hard sands of Daytona

Beach. Had one ever asked Frank how he thought his end would come, Frank could have told him. He had already worked it out in a makeshift basement laboratory over a year before his death. As usual, he had been right!

Who was Frank Lockhart? Back in the Roaring Twenties, he was a great national hero. He was one of the greatest racing drivers the world had seen. As a kid just out of his teens, jockeying a bucket of bolts, he became famous overnight as King of the Dirt Tracks. The first time he went near Indianapolis he won the 500-mile race spectacularly and decisively . . . in a borrowed car. When he rode the Championship circuit after that, he was consistently fantastic, winning races and smashing records from coast to coast. His name was almost as much a household word as that of Babe Ruth or Jack Dempsey even before he decided to become the fastest man on earth.

Then he built the Stutz Black Hawk, America's challenger for the land-speed record. Compared with the English record-holder, Seagrave's gigantic Sunbeam, the Black Hawk was a mere toy. But experts called it "the most mechanically perfect automobile ever built in the world" and predicted that what it lacked in size it would more than make up for in efficiency.

The eyes of the world were on Lockhart when, at the age of 25, he *did* go faster than man ever had gone on land. In 1928, 225 mph was as unprecedented for an automobile as 425 is today. But Lockhart had done it, the papers said. They also told in their stories of how a tire had blown at that speed and how the tiny car had rolled and banged eerily down the beach until, by a cruel, ironic stroke of fate, his broken body was flung at the feet of his waiting wife.

Where the Lockhart legend survives it has a mythically heroic quality. Illiterate, the hero's intellect was awesome. Obscure, he rocketed to world fame. Penniless, he raced his way to wealth. Frail, his endurance was unmatched. What other men accomplished with a lot, Lockhart surpassed with less. Horatio Alger never dared to invent such a hero—a little guy who slew giants by virtue of nothing but guts, infinite labor, and, above all, brains.

Legend though it is, it's not far from the truth. Lockhart did all these things. But he didn't do them all single-handedly, as the myth relates. Nor were the sacrifices and heartbreaks all his own.

Frank Lockhart stood five feet, three inches, weighed about 135 lbs., and had hazel eyes and flaxen hair. He was born in Dayton, Ohio, in 1903. Three years later he was spending all his waking hours in a nearby livery stable, watching automobiles of the day being worked on. If there was an eggbeater in the house, or any other mechanism, Frank appropriated it for his own.

When Frank was six, his father died and his mother moved with Frank and his brother Bob to California. She took in sewing to keep the family alive. It wasn't easy and they moved often.

Frank could not play with other kids; he had no patience with their aimless frivolity. He just worked on things, built things, and devoured all the reading matter he could find that dealt with things mechanical. He never had time to be bothered with spelling: as an adult he spelled sugar *shougar,* with phonetic logic. Even as a child he loved mathematics and felt far more at home with numbers than with words.

When Frank was eight he built a coaster—a soapbox-derby sort of thing that all the kids were building at the time. He couldn't get canvas or slats or tin to cover it, so he used tar paper. In neighborhood races he almost always won, mainly because he had the willpower to get the greatest number of kids to push him. Anyone who associated with Frank had to submit to his will. When his shoes needed polishing, Frank took care of one shoe and his brother did the other. And when Frank was running race cars, anyone who dropped in at the garage couldn't just sit and talk; he was handed a rag or a tool and put to work.

Frank had nothing but trouble in school. He had a mind that was totally his own and would work at nothing that was not important to him, personally. When automobiles still were being built with acetylene headlamps, Frank would spend his classroom time drawing cars with fully streamlined bodies. Teachers would brandish sheaves of these, demanding that his mother punish her child . . . help to get him away from this nonsense and down to serious studies. But Frank had long since convinced her that automobiles had to evolve toward the streamlined form. When he miraculously graduated from high school—to the merciful relief of all concerned—the principal told Carrie Lockhart that he had never been taken advantage of (meaning "treated as an equal") by a student as he had been by Frank.

By the time he was 16 Frank had to have a car, family poverty notwithstanding. He lived in Inglewood then, and a vegetable peddler named Gentle listened to the kid's hopes.

"I've got an old Model T chassis in my yard over in Boyle Heights," he said, "You can have it if you can get it home."

At that time Frank felt that anyone who would build a chassis from iron rather than from light hardwood was a fool. But here was the foundation for a car that he could own, now. Day after day he and his brother made the 12-mile trek on foot, carrying or dragging the T chassis home piece by piece.

Frank hung around all the speed shops, but his favorite was Ray McDowell's in Hollywood. McDowell—who later won fame as a builder of racing engines and components—gave him a junk T engine. Frank got it home and rebuilt it on his mother's kitchen floor.

"Our house wasn't like other people's," she told me. "That's how he started. McDowell was really a father to my Frank. He finally said, 'Bring all of your plunder to my place.' He had a pit. And they got that Ford so it would go. That was his first car. He ran it as Ascot and nobody ever passed him. He made no money there worth mentioning. He'd come home with burned feet and so tired that he couldn't get his shoes off. But that was what he had to do. He lived on grease and iron."

He lived to go fast. He never touched a drink or smoked or swore, not so much for any moral reason as for the fact that he considered these activities wasteful and pointless. He went with one girl in his life: the girl he married. In his human relationships he was fantastically stingy, but he would cheerfully spend his last cent to get a job done. That's what money was for.

Frank was no sentimentalist. "One day in '22," his mother recalls, "he came home and announced that he had to have five new tires for the Ford. I reminded him that we didn't have the $125—we hardly had a cent. He said, 'Well the furniture is paid for and you own some equity in the house—borrow the money.' I did. Frank wasn't a boy that you could say no to. His demands were very great."

After he got out of high school, Frank continued his education at a technical night school and by a lot of reading at home. He was shy, quiet, and well-liked. "Everybody loved Frank," his mother says, "for his intelligence. He didn't have idle talk in him. When he talked you listened, because you'd never heard it before. Maybe you've known someone like that; they're rare."

Somehow Frank came to the attention of the California Institute of Technology, and he was invited to take entrance examinations. He did, and shortly thereafter his mother was called to the office of Nobel Prize-winning physicist Robert Milliken.

"Your son's score in these tests is one of the highest in our experience," he said. "He has the mind of a born scientist. Can't you find someone to back his education?"

Carrie didn't have to think for long. "We don't know anyone like that," she answered. "But I'll do all your family's sewing if that will help."

Frank did not attend Cal Tech.

The first real racing car—a McDowell-Ford conversion run at Legion Ascot Speedway.

Instead, he kept driving at Ascot and other small west coast tracks. Once in a while someone would beat him, but never when there was any good money at stake. Ernie Olson, one of the finest racing mechanics we've ever produced, used to watch him there. "No one ever sat in a race car like Frank," he recalls. "On a mile dirt track he seemed to begin his slide in the middle of the straightaway; nobody ever imitated him. His skill and daring were tremendous. He wasn't exactly cool. He always got real bad butterflies before a race; he'd even vomit. In the car he'd say, 'Pat me on the shoulder.' You'd do that and it seemed to fix the butterflies. But once the flag fell he was in command of everything. I once asked him what he thought about when he was racing. 'All I think of from one second to the next,' he told me, 'is how to drive to win.'"

Hoping for a start in the big time, Frank wandered back to Indianapolis in 1926. He looked up the one man he knew

there, Ernie Olson, who was then in charge of the Bennet Hill's
Miller. It was arranged for Frank to take a few practice laps
on this course, one he had never seen before. The 23-year-old
dirt-tracked the bricks, taking the turns in full, controlled
slides, as the birds on the outside rail cringed. "My God," said
Hill, "that punk's getting around faster than I do."

When Lockhart came in Olson got him in a corner and
asked hom he liked the ride. "Fine, but I never was really on
it" was the answer. Olson then asked how fast Frank thought
he could get around the big oval if he tried. "Oh, about 4
seconds quicker," he said. That would have been a new track
record and Olson said, "Kid, if Benny needs relief, you've
got a ride in the race."

But the day before the race another Miller pilot, Steve
Kreis, was taken ill and Frank was offered his car. Newspapers
reported:

"The race was a quarter over and the name of Lockhart
burned every wire when a fine rain swept the brick saucer
clean of dirt and in its stead deposited a slippery, slimy surface
that drove veteran after veteran into the pits. The pace slowed
—for all except Lockhart, who seemed to drive his foot farther
into the floorboards."

When the race was called at 400 miles because of the rain,
the unknown kid from the west was 5 miles in front of his
nearest competition. It was one of the most dramatic victories
ever seen at the Speedway, and Frank was the talent discovery
of that or any year. Harry Miller came to him and offered him
a car for the rest of the season. This was praise from Caesar,
but Lockhart would not accept this fulfillment of his ambition
until he had the promise of the help of the best mechanic he
knew: Olson.

They made a nearly invincible team. Olson was a brainy
engineer in his own right as well as being a master mechanic,
race strategist, and major domo of equipment. But Lockhart
needed him not so much for his exceptional know-how—Frank

knew all the answers—as for his ability to keep pace with Frank's ideas and to help translate them into action. For Olson, it was an unforgettable privilege to be a principal figure in the revolution that Lockhart brought to American racing. "When any part failed or gave trouble," he recalls, "Frank would say, 'There's a reason for this. Let's find out what it is.' He might sit and study the problem for 3 or 4 days before doing a thing. But then he'd have the answer."

Valves broke regularly in the racing engines of the day. Frank figured out why, and to him must go the credit for today's situation, in which few, if any, valves ever break. Everyone used differentials on paved tracks until Frank started winning with a locked rear end, which everyone uses today. Everyone was content with torque tubes until Lockhart discovered that rear axle housings were bending under load. Now everyone uses truss rods or radius rods, as he did. Lockhart experimented constantly and carried an elaborate machine shop with him from track to track. What Miller and Duesenberg considered their best, he refined to the nth degree.

Lockhart has been credited with the invention of the supercharger intercooler, but this was really not one of his original contributions. While working on his car at Miller's plant in Los Angeles in the summer of '26, he became acquainted with John Weisel, a young Cal Tech engineering student who spent his vacations in Miller's employ. When Lockhart tried to interest Miller in detail improvements on his masterpieces, the Old Man was scornful. So Lockhart hired Weisel to help him with design and drafting problems and through John met his brother, Zenas, who recently had obtained his degree in mechanical engineering. His master's thesis had been a study of the supercharging of aircraft engines.

It was Zenas who proposed the intercooler. Here is how it happened: Frank had the excellent idea of building a gear train which could be bolted to the top of the transmission of his Buick road car and could be used for testing superchargers at racing revs, anywhere and at any time. Zenas proposed a refinement: design a dynamometer into the device so as to be able to tell with precision the effect of any change in blower setup. It was at this time that Zenas explained his intercooler theory to Frank. With Frank's Buick engine turning over at 1450 rpm and, through the transmission, driving the blower at the equivalent of 7500 crankshaft revolutions, Weisel asked Frank to feel the blast from the blower outlet. From 18 inches away it was like touching a red-hot bar. Weisel said, "I can design an air-cooled manifold for you that will get rid of a lot of that heat. If it doesn't give you another eight mph you won't owe me a dime." The first time out with the new setup, Lockhart's Miller went 8.5 mph faster than it ever had before.

That was at the Culver City board track on Mar. 6, 1927. Frank took one warm-up lap in his 91 cubic-inch Miller, then raised his hand to signal to the starter that he was on his way, and turned in an all-time record of 144.2 mph.

The intercooler was a secret. The car's hood was kept locked and was never raised until hidden from unauthorized eyes. Frank drove the big-time circuit from coast to coast and dominated almost every race he entered. In one afternoon at Cleveland, for example, he broke over 100 records for the mile dirt track, including de Palma's from 1 to 25 miles and Milton's from 50 to 100 miles. The intercooler was kept secret for almost a year.

That season Lockhart and Olson took their much-modified Miller 91 to Roberts Dry Lake in the Mojave Desert—the car long since had been purchased from Miller, who would not tolerate design changes being made on *his* car. Lockhart ran for official straightaway records under AAA sanction. Said a newspaper account, "Shattering all records for the 91-inch class at 171.02 mph—the fastest time made by any car in the world excepting the Daytona monster, thirty times larger. Lockhart's two-way average against a heavy cross wind was

He could hardly write his own language, yet such was the genius of Lock-hart that he could design machinery like the Stutz-Blackhawk engine.

164.85 mph. The new record, made by a midget with the power of a giant, is a startling achievement when compared with the records established during recent years by cars with motors many times its size."

In '27, Lockhart came within an ace of winning the Indianapolis 500 for the second year in a row. He held the lead for 300 miles, and then a con rod broke. After that, he redesigned Miller's rods. He finished the season a wealthy man. His lap winnings alone at Indy: $11,000.

Among the millions who had been following every step of Lockhart's blazing career with fascinated admiration was Fred E. Moskovics. His family had moved to the United States from Budapest when Moskovics was only four. His father had been a mining engineer and F. E. took a degree in mechanical engineering. He grew up with the automobile and with racing. He had managed the Mercedes team in the first Vanderbilt Cup Race, gotten Ralph de Palma his first ride in a race car and, after taking over as president of Stutz in the mid-Twenties, he put that marque back in the racing business both in America and in Europe.

Moskovics' enthusiasm was boundless when he learned that Lockhart had beaten the previous year's land-speed record with a tiny car of American manufacture. He sought the kid out and got to know him well.

Says Moskovics who, in his seventies, does his commuting in a 300SL, "Frank was the greatest natural mechanic I've ever come in contact with. He told me of his ambition to win the land-speed record for the United States. I knew that if anyone could do it, Lockhart could. I agreed to give him all the backing in my power. I got a group of wealthy sportsmen together who put up about $20,000. He agreed to call his machine the Stutz Black Hawk, and I was able to add another $15,000 and put the facilities of the Stutz factory in Indianapolis at his disposal."

Olson, in the meantime, had been working hard to arrange Lockhart's participation in the Italian Grand Prix at Monza. "I had the deal wrapped up," he says, "when Frank told me he was going to build the beach car. I didn't exactly have a premonition of disaster. I just got physically ill. I felt it was the wrong thing to do and began to look for another job."

Lockhart wired the Weisel brothers, asking them to come to Indianapolis to work on the project at a guaranteed salary for a minimum of four months. The challenge was fascinating to them. They hurried east and followed Lockhart around the country as he kept up with his racing commitments.

"My brother and I," says Zenas, "traveled with a suitcase each of clothes and a big trunk filled with books and instruments and a drawing board. We landed in Indianapolis, went with Frank to Altoona, then to Salem where we got the car pretty well in mind, then to Buffalo, then to Detroit, then back to Indianapolis. Unusual working conditions. I can still remember him sitting in a chair in a hotel room while I measured his seated posture and laid out the frame kickups so they would just clear his elbows. We built the car around him."

Lockhart's idea was to attack the record with a car running two separate Miller 91's geared together after the fashion of Milton's LSR Duesenberg. He also planned on using a bug-shaped envelope body. Zenas' engineering training had included heavy emphasis on aerodynamics as well as engine design. In this case, both were closely related, and he produced drawings of the Bugatti 16-cylinder aircraft engine to show how a pair of straight eighths could be joined in a very compact manner by integrating them into a single crankcase.

Concerned with the smallest possible frontal area for the car, Zenas squelched the envelope-body approach: it would sacrifice more than the meager available horsepower could afford. He held out for exposed wheels and for a torpedo shape that would enclose everything within the frame. Thus, not one square millimeter of frontal area would be allowed to absorb thrust that otherwise could be converted into speed.

Zenas streamlined the axles, of course. He also streamlined the wheels that were sitting raggedly out in the air. He had listened to drivers who had run at high speeds and were unhappy with the handling of disc-covered wire wheels. He reasoned that the effect of cross winds on their steering was not due entirely to the lateral load created by the wind acting against the area of the wheel discs and pushing them in the direction of the wind. Zenas felt that the unexpectedly strong effects that had been noted were due, at least in part, to the fact that at high speeds the disc wheel, if inclined at an angle, became a lifting surface similar to an airplane wing. He also reasoned that the center of pressure on such a wheel was well ahead of the kingpin, adding leverage to the tendency to steer in the direction of cross winds. So Weisel designed the streamlined wheel spats for the Black Hawk and made them long. He calculated their shape so that (1) the center of pressure would be well aft of the kingpins, counteracting somewhat the car's tendency to steer in the direction of a cross wind and (2) acting as air rudders, they would contribute to the car's directional stability.

That was the philosophy behind the spats, which always were essentially parallel to the car's long axis. Calculations indicated that, with an anticipated coefficient of friction on the beach of .5, the front wheels could not be turned more than 0 degrees, 6 minutes, without throwing the car into a skid. The lock-to-lock arc was fixed just short of that figure; total movement at the rim of the 14-inch steering wheel was just one quarter of an inch.

Efforts had been made in the past to give racing and record cars a streamlined outward appearance, but their undersides and engine spaces were left ragged. To cut down this rather large source of wind drag, Weisel enclosed the underside of the car and sealed off the engine compartment from outside air, except for small intake and exhaust openings. He originated the idea of eliminating the conventional radiator from straightaway machines. Coolant for the Black Hawk's power plant circulated through an 8-pound ice tank.

The tiny 181.6-cubic-inch engine was supercharged, of course, and was fitted with intercoolers. The intercooler on the speedway car had been mounted under the car's hood, and its effectiveness depended upon the flow of air through the engine compartment. For the record machine, Weisel designed an entirely new kind of intercooler: a delicate, filigree-like aluminum casting contoured to follow perfectly the surface of the car's skin.

The basic idea was to enclose all parts of the machine while still avoiding the obvious tactic of wrapping it in a con-

Lockhart, in the Miller Special, after winning the 1926 Indianapolis 500.

tinuous envelope. To get the body as small as possible, while enclosing everything but axles and wheels, called for an extremely narrow frame and for springs that would also be located within the body shell. Given these conditions, the springs as well as the frame rails had to be extremely close together, a fact which would not help stability with regard to torsional action of the front axle.

To get the springs within the minimum-area body, they had to be only 11 inches apart. Weisel wanted to tie the axles to the chassis without even a thousandth of an inch of mechanical play, so that the car could be steered without concern for any movement between these elements. He designed and patented a unique suspension system. Each spring was a double cantilever machined from a solid-steer billet. The front ends of the front springs were bolted to a steel spool, which served as the center section of the front axle. The stub axles, in turn, were bolted to this assembly outboard of the springs; the back ends of the springs were bolted to bronze spacer blocks, which were bolted to the frame. Total spring deflection was three quarters of an inch, during which the kingpins remained parallel with the frame.

The rear springs were of the same unusual construction; their front ends were bolted solidly to the frame, and their rear ends pivoted around the rear-axle housing. The worm-gear final drive was dictated, not by Stutz sponsorship of the project, but by the fact that this feature permitted lowering the car's height by about 6 inches.

It seems that the Black Hawk was the first car in the United States to make extensive use of wind-tunnel testing. The base line for the record machine was Frank's 91-inch speedway car and the knowledge that it had turned 171 mph at 7200 rpm. Therefore, a precise scale model of the 91 was built, complete with radiator opening, dummy engine under the hood, hood louvers, knock-off hubs, dummy driver—all the features that might contribute to wind drag. An equally precise model of the Black Hawk was also made. Utilizing the known top speed of the 91 and the data obtained by wind-tunnel tests, the approximate available horsepower of both engines could be calculated . . . and so could the terminal velocity of the Black Hawk.

Bear in mind that the fastest car in the world at this time was Seagrave's huge Sunbeam. It weighed 8000 lbs., had a 2760-cubic-inch, 1000 bhp engine and held the world's two-way record at 203.790 mph.

Lockhart's Black Hawk weighed just under 2800 lbs. This may sound light but, because the car was a rather small one, its density-weight in relation to size—was great. Its 181-cubic-inch engine was assumed to deliver 525 bhp to the rear wheels at 7500 rpm. Thorough wind-tunnel tests were conducted by the Curtiss Airplane Company, whose engineers credited the little car with a potential top speed of 283 mph.

The models were then sent to the Army wind tunnel at Wright Field for double checking. There, the top speed was calculated to be 281 mph. But by this time Lockhart, still racing in every championship event, had his 91 turning 8200 rpm on the board-track straightaways. The horsepower estimate had to be revised upward and final calculations indicated that, on gasoline, the Black Hawk was good for 330 mph! Methanol had not yet been discovered in the United States as a racing fuel.

Naturally, no word of this fantastic potential was allowed to go beyond those persons most intimately concerned with the car. Even Moskovics seems to have had no inkling of it. But Zenas Weisel still has the records.

Standard strategy among record breakers was and is not to exceed existing records by extravagant margins but, rather, to top them adequately, reap the rewards, rest on the laurels until a new record is established, and then, if the potential of your machine has not been exhausted, go back and break the record again. Lockhart's plan was to boost the land-speed record to about 225 mph, and most of his equipment tests were based on this simulated speed, including tire tests.

Jean Marcenac was in charge of the "inner sanctum" in the basement of the Stutz plant where the beach car was built. He helped Frank run the tire tests. The test rig consisted of a big Stutz straight-eight engine, bolted to a concrete foundation, which drove the shaft on which the wheels and tires were spun. Finally, the time for the destruction test. The shop was cleared, and the test tire, inflated to 125 psi, was set spinning at the equivalent of 225 mph. Marcenac and Lockhart shrank behind concrete columns, and Frank fired at the tire with a shotgun. The tremendous, unbalanced forces that were suddenly released tore the heavy engine from the block, and its aft end disintegrated. Lockhart grimly said, "Well, I'm done for if a tire blows." He was depressed for days, but eventually accepted the gamble.

In February of 1928, less than 8 months after the pre-
liminary paperwork on the Black Hawk was completed, the
car was finished and ready to go. The $35,000 with which the
project had been launched did not go far, and the beach car
gradually drained off a large percentage of Lockhart's massive
racing winnings. Estimates of its total cost run as high as
$100,000. As Lockhart's investment in the project rose beyond
all expectations, his concern necessarily swung more and more
from the pure challenge of ultimate speed to the financial
relief and reward that would come once the record was in his
hands. The project took on a definitely commercial character,
and Frank and his manager would spend long hours comput-
ing the eventual take from track and vaudeville appearances,
product endorsements, and awards from manufacturers.

Money became all-important to this extent: Lockhart had
always driven on Firestone racing tires and had used them in
his tests at the Stutz factory. But a new tire manufacturer
offered him $20,000 if he would set the new record using this
firm's experimental high-speed tires. He accepted.

Just before his final attack on the record, Frank's mother
wrote him. "I told him that I was very ill and almost desperate.

*Prelude to disaster: Frank in the Stutz makes his last run down the Beach
at 200 plus.*

. . . suddenly the right rear tire shreds and the car leaps into the air . . .

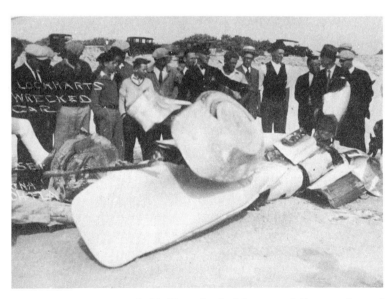

. . . to come to rest, a tangled ball of what had been carefully crafted metal.

Would he send me just $10? It would make all the difference in the world. A couple of days before the run I got a wire from him. He didn't mention the money. It just said, 'Ma, I have the world by the horns. You'll never have to push a needle again. I'll never have to work any more.' "

The Black Hawk was shipped to Daytona early in February, and practice runs began. Day after day they ran, but could not get above 180 mph. Frank was in a frenzy. Finally, with Moskovics' help, they found their trouble: laminar flow across the supercharger inlets was starving the engine for air. Small scoops at the inlets transformed the car's performance. But by this time the weather had become increasingly bad, and the AAA timers were ready to pick up and leave. They would stay just one more day: for Washington's birthday and the scheduled stock-car runs on the beach.

The weather was foul and the beach was miserable. But thousands of paid admissions had been collected and, in spite of intermittent rain all day long, the crowds stayed to see if Lockhart would run. Finally, late in the afternoon, the little white car was towed to the south end of the course. The next thing the crowd was aware of was the 40,000-rpm scream of the Black Hawk's superchargers. He was on it all the way, touching between 220 and 225, when he hit a patch of rain. He couldn't see and the car edged into soft sand. Then a crash, two end-over-end flips, and a flight into the sea. The car landed on its belly and then skipped like a stone over the water, making slow barrel rolls in the air. It came to rest, wheels down, nearly submerged in the surf.

It seemed impossible that Lockhart could be alive. The crowd surged toward the wreck. As the first wave lapped over the car, a hand appeared above the water. "Save him . . . he'll drown." Lockhart was pinned in the cockpit, but twenty men rushed into the waves and dragged the car to shore. Aside from shock—he had a congenital fear of water—his only injury was, miraculously, a couple of cut tendons in his right hand.

Moskovics says, "The car looked like a ruin, but actually it wasn't badly damaged. We shipped it back to Indianapolis for repair. I did everything in the world to keep Frank from going back to the beach that year. But he had made no end of commitments, and I guess he had to go."

In mid-April, Lockhart and the Black Hawk were back at Daytona with the eyes of the world on them. It was at dawn on the 25th that he made his first sally, a warm-up to the south. The beach was perfect, and he returned north a little faster. Then south again, with the superchargers' scream announcing that he was getting down to business. Then he began his fourth run, really flying. He was just about to enter the traps when a spray of sand shot from his right rear tire and the car came smashing, tumbling, thudding down the beach, and that was the end.

Officials who examined the evidence before the tide came in said that in braking at the end of his third run Frank had locked his rear wheels for about 100 feet. In that long slide, Frank had very likely slit or otherwise weakened a tire on a piece of hidden flotsam or a sea shell. On the final run that tire had blown with just the results that Lockhart had predicted after his shotgun test.

Part II

THE BUILDERS:
Men Behind the Men Behind the Wheel

There are motorcar manufacturers and there are motorcar builders. The manufacturer is merely content to bolt together a product which he hopes to sell to as many people as possible. The motorcar builder also hopes to sell a product, but in each one of his wares he builds a little of himself.

There have not been many of the latter breed—at least not in the last few decades—five, perhaps; at the most, ten. Who hasn't heard of Ettore Bugatti, the sculptor turned auto builder, whose cars have inspired such fanatic loyalty among their owners that even today, almost 50 years after the first one was built, the club comprised of these owners keeps a pedigree of every known car in existence. There have been other craftsmen, perhaps not as inspired as *Le Patron,* who also have given of themselves and their talents in such a way as to have made a unique mark on automotive history.

In America, the car builder has given away almost completely to the manufacturer. In England and on the continent, particularly in Italy, he still holds his own. On the following pages you will meet two Englishmen and an Italian who still feel that building automobiles is a personal business.

5. Sixty Fast Years
by Maynard Lewis

"I don't know how he does it. Every time he makes a move it's a winner." The speaker was an executive of a large foreign-car importing firm and he was speaking of a short, balding man whose beaming smile and healthy tan is familiar to everyone with the slightest knowledge of sports cars. That man is, of course, Donald Healey. More than sixty years young, Healey only recently stormed over the salt beds at Bonneville at 200 miles an hour in one of his own modified sports cars. At an age when most men in his financial position would retire, Healey is busy designing newer and better cars. Healy has a near-genius for designing cars that other people *like*. He also has a flair for designing cars that people can *buy*. Nearly everyone of his models has, indeed, been a winner in the sales-record derby. Both Healey and the mighty British Motor Corporation, which assembles and distributes the cars, are known the world over. Donald Healey likes cars as an enthusiast likes cars. Actually, when he does anything, from water skiing to designing, it is with the utmost enthusiasm. Perhaps the only way to sum up this many-faceted, happy man is to say that Donald Healey is *alive*.

In his early sixties, and with three decades of race and competition driving behind him, Donald Mitchell Healey has reached an age and a position where many men would be content to let their bellies outgrow their chests and to start thinking in the past tense. But with Healey, designer and co-maker of one of the world's most successful sports cars, it is otherwise. As a businessman he moves so fast that, in the

words of one of his staff, "you have to get in his slipstream to
keep up with him." In the records field his future endeavors
are bent on beating 300 mph with an Austin-Healey of 3 liters
displacement—with himself as driver, naturally.

If he brings it off, this will make him the fastest sexagenarian on wheels, easily; and unless Donald Campbell gets
in first with the land-speed record he's planning, Healey will
also be one of only two triple centurions alive. The other is
Captain George Eyston.

The life of Donald Healey is lived, metaphorically speaking, in cable-car transit from one peak of ambition to another.
He had always hankered, for instance, to drive at 200 miles
per hour; and in due course he did so, turning 200.9 mph for
the two-way mile at Bonneville in August of 1956, using a
prototype Austin-Healey 100-6 with supercharger and *renn-
limousin* body. With this target attained he could have quite
easily shaken the salt from his feet forever and resolved to
begin being his age. The fact is, however, that he *isn't* his
age by any yardstick except the calendar; and so, true to temperament, he quietly transmuted this yesterday's ambition
into today's steppingstone.

Of course, there is some rational justification for pressing
on to three hundred. That 200.9 mph, although a spanking
clip for a sports car derivative of only 2.6 liters capacity and
based upon so unpretentious an engine as BMC's C-type,
didn't cause the FIA to bat an eyelid; the international Class
D record for the flying mile still stands where it has stood
since 1939—at 248.3 mph, clocked by Rudolf Caracciola (V-12
Mercedes-Benz) on a German autobahn.

With disarming honesty, Donald Healey admits that
sprints achieved with the aid of supercharging and a radically
nonstandard body shape are practically meaningless as a cri-
terion of his production wares. He undertakes them, he says,
simply because in the United States, where most of his output
is sold, the publicity impact is useful. The British are less

Donald Healey.

impressionable in such matters—if a figure isn't specifically a record, they just don't want to know about it.

Once you start adding blowers, roofing in cockpits, and extending noses and tails to lengths that wouldn't conceivably be acceptable on a road car, you might just as well take leave of the original blueprint entirely, Mr. Healey plausibly argues. Accordingly, the next Austin-Healey migrant to Bonneville will probably have the driver's turret out ahead of the front-wheel centers, à la Cobb, and be powered by a new engine giving around 450 horsepower and closely crowding the 3-liter limit. This would represent an increase of 150 bhp over the 1956 output with blower. Whether the top end of the projected engine will retain a resemblance to the current Hundred powerplant remains to be seen, but the extra displacement sought cannot be attained with the existing cylinder centers. In other words, this isn't just an overboring operation.

On and off, Healey has tinkered with the idea of a prone driver position for his short-distance record car, and it may be that the new edition will follow this recipe for minimal cross section.

According to him, the aerodynamic shape of the 1956 sprinter left plenty to be desired, but not all the evidence points that way. Three or four times, it may be remembered, backfires caused the blower drive chain to break at speed. Once the breakage occurred a quarter-mile short of the trap. Coasting, Donald's timed average through the mile was better than 150 mph.

In contrast with the man who first drove over the brine at 300 mph (Campbell, 1935), Healey emphatically plays down the danger potential of such speeds on the salt. In fact, he says, it is the inherently high safety factor, and the very small physical exertion called for, that driving is not too dangerous up to, and if need be exceeding, 300 an hour. His one cardinal rule in this context is to let the car go where it wants to if a side wind hits it. The room is there, and then is the time to use up a bit of it.

The name Healey, originally standing on its own and later hyphenated with Nash and Austin, is identified with such striking success, both commercially and in various forms of speedwork, that it's difficult to realize that Donald's career as a car manufacturer only dates back to 1946. But personally, in association with a series of established British marques, he had made a reputation as a hard-headed and resourceful competition driver long before setting up as a constructor on his own account shortly after World War II. As a Royal Flying Corps pilot in the First World War, he hoped to make aviation his peacetime profession, but a flying crash and the resulting injuries enforced a change of plan. He left the RFC and returned to his birthplace, a townlet called Perranporth on the coast of Cornwall, England, where he bought himself a garage business. From this base he participated in the leading English trials of the '20s, serving a promising apprenticeship at the wheel of an ABC, a sprightly light car with two horizontal air-cooled cylinders, like half a VW. He also drove this little two-banger at the old Brooklands track.

From the ABC, Donald graduated to a Triumph Seven, unrecognizable ancestor of today's TR3, and subsequently rang changes on later and larger Triumphs, Rileys, and Invictas. When the Royal Automobile Club put on its first rally in England in 1928, foreshadowing a later British boom in this type of competition, Healey and his Triumph Seven won it outright. Encouraged, he raised his sights and took a bash at the Monte Carlo marathon the following January, getting his wheels in the groove for a run of Monte success that no other Briton has yet equalled—between 1929 and the outbreak of World War II his score in Europe's toughest competition included one straight win, one second place, one third, one first in the separate light-car category, and the only recorded instance of a car being cut clean in half by a freight train. The London *Motor* has described Donald as "all-time's greatest British contestant of *Le Rallye* . . . an ideal compound of resource, skill, guile, and toughness."

In the light of his career on the Monte Carlo trail, it isn't surprising that Healey regards record breaking at multiple-century speeds as a tame and sedentary occupation. It may be that he himself has lost count of the number of times he has escaped pulverization by a gnat's whisker in the rally, but the most miraculous of these near-misses was certainly his 1935 adventure on a Danish grade crossing. Driving a supercharged Triumph Dolomite straight-eight through a pitch-dark night, with patches of mist to make driving even trickier, his ear caught a sound that he took to denote a seizure of the blower. What he didn't know was that seizing Dolomite blowers sounded exactly like Danish freight-train sirens, and vice versa. The impact, when it came, was oblique, and literally bifurcated the Triumph about 9-inches ahead of the windshield. The front half of the auto, including the engine and the rest of the hood's contents, was ground to fragments. The back half, containing Healey and his navigator, was gently side-swiped out of harm's way and *didn't even capsize!* The navigator shook his head and one tooth fell out. Otherwise, nobody got a scratch.

The *Motor,* in extolling Healey's skill and guile as a rally-man, wasn't just playing with words. In 1931, the year he won the Monte, his 4½-liter Invicta ran off the road soon after leaving Stavanger, his Norwegian starting point, and cut a telegraph pole down to bumper height. The blow threw the whole chassis out of line, giving the steering a powerful bias a-port and leaving one front brake for dead. Under these handicaps, Donald and his co-driver not only made it to Monte on time over 1,700 miles of snow and icebound roads, but Healey himself beat the entire field in the decisive eliminating test on arrival: of all things, a braking test.

The following year the decider took the form of a top-gear flexibility test. Finding nothing in the regulations to forbid such a maneuver, Healey had a pair of dime-size back wheels and tires shipped down to Monte in advance and fitted them to his Invicta before showing for the test. These wheels were so small that, with the tires flat, the chassis touched the ground. On his trans-European performance he was favorably placed to win the rally outright for the second time running, but it happened that Vaselle, one of the Hotchkiss factory's Monte Carlo virtuosi, had stopped off at his sponsors' Paris plant and switched to an ultralow axle ratio. This even smarter dodge enabled Vaselle to beat Healey on so-called flexibility and thereby win the rally.

Final tests, in which even seasoned operators are liable to be afflicted with agonizing stage fright, always found Donald as happy as a baby in a pram. His serenity and detachment preceding and during these ordeals was the wonder and envy of mercurial Latin rivals and accounted for much of his success as a rally driver. In addition to his Monte Carlo prizes, he also won both the Austrian and Hungarian alpine trials for Invicta.

Healey returned to his old love, flying, in the Second World War—commanding a regional wing of the Air Training Corps in England. He used any leisure his ATC duties afforded to work up designs for the car that was to carry his name, pooling his own down-to-earth practicality with the advanced technical and theoretical knowledge of an old friend, Achilles Sampietro. Sampietro had been an associate of Georges Roesch, designer of the classic Talbots in this company's pre-Rootes era, and is now with Willys-Overland.

The Healey prototype, powered by a slightly warmed version of the 2½-liter Riley engine, was on road test 3 months after V-J Day and went into small scale production during 1946. In its three variants—roadster, sedan, and convertible—this Riley-based car kept Donald's little factory busy until 1952, when the need for increased dollar business led to the introduction of the Anglo-U.S. half-caste known as the Nash-Healey.

By dint of a roof line that discouraged the wearing of hats

by those in the back seat, plus a general contouring that wasn't far behind the Italian thinking of the day, the Healey 2½ sedan achieved a low over-all drag factor. This was effectively demonstrated when, soon after the original launching, it hit an independently timed speed of 104 mph on an Italian *autostrada* of far from perfect surface, thereby establishing itself as the world's fastest stock passenger car. (Stock *models* had, of course, exceeded this speed before the war, both in Europe and the United States, but the ones in question were not still in production).

Healey happened to be in Italy at the time of the first postwar Mille Miglia, in June of 1947, and the fact that the winning Alfa, driven by Biondetti and Romano, averaged the relatively modest speed of 69.58 mph, sent him off into a brown study. The upshot of these musings was that he led a three-car expeditionary force to Brescia for the race in '48. Donald himself, sharing a roadster model with his eldest son, Geoffrey, finished ninth on general classification, averaging over 100 miles per hour for a 150-mile stretch of *autostrada;* Count Johnny Lurani headed the whole touring category, irrespective of displacement, with a Healey sedan; the third car in the team broke its transmission. Another closed Healey, stoked by Tommy Wisdom, the well-known British motoring writer, again pulled off the touring class in the next year's MM.

Don has driven in five postwar Mille Miglia—a stoutish effort for a man who was in his fiftieth year before he even learned his way around the mighty Brescia-Rome-Brescia lap. It was in the 1953 race, at the wheel of a Nash-Healey hardtop, that he hit a bridge parapet at 90, ejecting his co-driver through the windshield. The pane, which was, fortunately, framed in rubber, didn't put up a lethal resistance.

Staunchly pro-American, Healey takes pride in the fact that it was his product that first whetted Briggs Cunningham's appetite for racing. Briggs' personal debut in speedwork was made in a Silverstone Healey with a Cadillac V-8 engine fitted in place of the regular Riley four-lunger; prolonged experiments with this combination preceded the establishment of Cunningham as a marque in its own right.

When the idea of welding a big-displacement American powerplant to his own chassis first occurred to Healey, he had his eye on the Cadillac V-8 engine. Tentatively, GM thought they might be able to make available the few units he'd need, and he was invited to Detroit to discuss the project with Charles Wilson, at that time president of General Motors. En route to New York by sea, Donald chanced to make the acquaintance of George Mason of Nash-Kelvinator. Drawn together by common interests, the travelers struck up a friendship. The object of Healey's trip eventually came out in conversation. Before they parted, Mason made it known that he would be happy to supply Nash engines, if the Cadillac *parleys* came to nothing. That was how Healey came to have his name hyphenated with Nash.

Although the Nash engine, being inferior to the Cad in both displacement and specific output, gave the Healey a performance that in retrospect seems not far removed from the bovine, it served its purpose adequately at the time. Highpoint of the Nash-Healey's career in sports-car racing was Le Mans, 1952, when a model driven by Wisdom and Johnson placed third, several parishes behind the two survivors from Stuttgart's threesome team of 300SL Mercs. From a commercial standpoint, the big advertising noise made in the U.S. by Nash-Kelvinator paved the way for the cut that Healey was later to make at the American cake with his smaller Austin-Healey Hundreds. About 1,200 Nash-Healeys were built, all but a handful of them going to the American market.

Without exercising any of the back-slapping winsomeness of a sycophant, Donald Healey somehow always seems preordained for support from the right friends at the right moment. A case in point was the way Sir Leonard Lord fell into his lap, so to speak, at the crucial moment of the debut

of the Healey Hundred. On his own initiative, and without
any effort at enlisting outside backing, Healey laid down an
all-new chassis and body design in the summer of 1952. For
this car, christened the 100, he had negotiated the purchase
from Austin of surplus A90 engines, as used in Longbridge's
already obsolete Atlantic hard-top. As head of Austin, Lord
was, of course, fully in accord with this transaction, but his
personal interest in it, right up to the time the 100 was un-
veiled at the annual London automobile exhibition in October, was rather low. Then, at the Earl's Court show, it happened. Lord came, saw, and was conquered. Convinced that
Healey held an ace, he immediately offered to transfer production of the 100 to Longbridge and put Austin's international distributive machinery to work on its behalf. The deal
was concluded almost overnight, and the car that had entered
the show hall as a Healey acquired its Austin prefix right
there on the stand.

This alliance transformed Healey's fortunes and scale of
operations, and during its 4-year lifespan the 4-cylinder 100
had the fairly unusual distinction of maintaining a demand
that constantly out-stripped supply. Fourteen thousand of

*The 200 m.p.h. Austin-Healey. At the age of 60, Donald Healey piloted
this missile fast enough to qualify for membership in the exclusive 200
Mile-an-Hour Club.*

Donald Healey, in white overalls and no hat, prepares to board the Austin-Healey 200 m.p.h. streamliner (Bonneville, 1955).

these brisk two-seaters were exported to the States, nourishing the BMC exchequer to the tune of $20,000,000. From the moment of the Lord-Healey handshake, Donald's small plant at Warwick, where all his earlier cars had been built, was relieved entirely of manufacturing and assembling processes. It is presently devoted to service, tuning for competitions, prototype development, and conversions from stock specification to the faster MM formula.

Of late, the marque has been busy producing Austin-Healey 100-6's, introduced in the Fall of 1956 to replace the four. From a performance standpoint there was perhaps an augury of future possibilities in the speeds put up in Utah by a special-bodied variant with three double-throat carburetors and a 9-1 compression ratio; figures for 200 miles and 500 kilometers, both breaking international class records, were above 152 mph.

As busy as a bird dog the whole day long, and therefore a happy man, Healey currently divides his time about equally between his car and powerboat interests. His transoceanic travels between Britain and the United States, which weren't exactly desultory when he only had cars on his mind, nowadays approach fan-belt tempo. Healey Marine, his boat enterprise, has beachheads in Canada and the Bahamas as well as in England, and is growing all the time. This company's products like those of its car associate, enable Donald to combine a business with a hobby; water skiing, one of the purposes for which his marine craft are designed, is a favorite diversion of his. Like record breaking on salt, he says, it is essentially safe because there isn't anything or anybody to run into, which makes it a hand-picked pastime for men of an age past their Monte Carlo prime.

6. Never Call Him Henry!
by Merwin Dembling

Perhaps the greatest asset any corporation can have is smooth cooperation among the heads of its various departments. Lotus Engineering, then, should be the smoothest, most efficient corporation in the world. The head of the corporation, its chief of design, the head of the racing department, and the head of sales think as one man, because one man occupies all these positions. His name is Colin Chapman, an apple-cheeked, intense young man who almost singlehandedly has revised the thinking of racing-car designers the world over. In an automotive variation on the "better mouse trap" theme, Chapman began in the decade after World War II to take advantage of the "do-it-yourself" trend in motor racing. At that time there was no ready-made equipment for the racing enthusiast—it was "do it yourself" or do without. Chapman stepped into the breach with a kit that enabled the enthusiast to do it himself better than his neighbor. So successful was this venture that those whose talents did not include the ability to put together such an advanced sort of Tinker Toy asked Colin to do it for them. The result was a succession of fantastically successful racing sports cars that took on all comers. It was also the beginning of what has become England's fastest, most spasmodically, growing motor-manufacturing concern.

Colin Chapman, the man behind the Lotus, is a plump, peppery, prematurely grey London engineer whose face occasionally sports the kind of smile found on cats who have eaten canaries.

Chapman has plenty to be smug about. In the years since he was a frustrated ex-fighter pilot banging around in trials with just another Austin-7 special, he has seen his Lotus cars win a coveted place for themselves high on the roster of hot sporting vehicles. From a man who had to do a lot of fast promoting to snag the engine out of a $100 wreck, he has become a businessman who can look his accountants unflinchingly in the eye. The final mark of authenticity was stamped on his success when Britain's starchy Society of Motor Manufacturers and Traders opened the doors of their Piccadilly palace to him. Still in his thirties, he's by far their youngest member.

Despite enough feathers in his cap to make him the closest thing to an Indian chief to be found in the North-London superb of Tottenham, Chapman birdles when referred to as a boy genius and positively snarls when overenthusiastic admirers rate him as a potential Henry Ford. Nevertheless, he and the late Mr. Ford have a couple of important traits in common. Chapman, like old Henry, has the uncanny kind of engineering talent that almost always turns up a simple solution to a complicated problem. Troubled with oversteer on his Austin-7 based Mark I Lotus, Chapman eliminated it neatly and brilliantly by turning the back axle upside down. Wanting a rigid chassis for fast roadwork and a supple one for trials, Chapman got both on his Mark II by inventing the "Jelly Joint," in which the front axle and spring were pivoted on a bracket. The loosening of two bolts let the entire assembly swing free to pick its way over rough terrain. Tightening the bolts gave the Mark II the stiff springing necessary to keep a high-speed car from ignoring the road. Needing four-port pep from the two-port Austin-7 engine, Chapman designed for his Mark III a canny inlet manifold, in which a center division nuzzled into an asbestos strip between two valves, giving each a private port.

Natural genius? Not altogether. Chapman is a product of

Colin Chapman in his factory in Hornsey.

the University of London's College of Engineering. He prefaced his entry into full-time motorcar design by reading every technical automotive treatise in the library of the Institute of Mechanical Engineers. His Jelly Joint was the result of a months-long study of tractor front suspensions. But the talent was there to begin with: at the age of seven he mopped up neighborhood competition by sawing a baby-carriage axle in half and equipping his soapbox racer with crude but adequate I.F.S.!

There is another gift that Chapman shares with Ford, and the world being the place it is, this may be the important one. Ford's ability to rake in gold was so spectacular that his heirs now have the chore of giving it away. Chapman hasn't gotten that far yet, but his financial skill is fast becoming legendary. One friend, who prefers not to be named, describes Chapman's business technique as a dazzling combination of charm and calculation. "Colin will sell you the right time," he says, "and probably get a commission from the chap who owns the watch!"

This type of money-making brain is normally found only in second-hand car dealers, so it's not much of a surprise to find that Chapman made his business debut in that field. He didn't set out to become a second-hand car dealer, but his first car—a decrepit B.S.A. three-wheeler—handled so badly that in one day he turned it over—at a $50 profit. This was such easy money that he couldn't resist getting into the business on a full-time basis. After a while, though, he took a position as a development engineer with the British Aluminium Corporation. His job was to dope out new uses for aluminum, but he is the kind of engineer who follows wherever his slide rule leads him: he never hesitated to recommend sheet steel when the figures turned out that way. The corporation showed remarkable patience: they kept him on the payroll until he turned in his uniform to head his own business—making Lotus cars.

Considering the amount of genuine fame the marque has won, and the size of the dent it has made in motor sport, it is a bit of a surprise to discover how few Lotuses there really are. The breakdown goes something like this:

MARK I—Chapman's original special—Austin-7 chassis and engine. Only one made.

MARK II—Austin-7 frame, Ford 1172-cc engine, and Chapman's Jelly-Joint. Trounced a Type-37 Bug at Silverstone in 1950. One only.

MARK III—Austin-7 frame and engine, with de-siamesed inlet ports. No other 750-cc formula car could touch it during the season Chapman raced it. Only one made.

MARK IV—The last Austin-based Lotus, and the first Lotus made to sell. The orders poured in after Chapman's dazzling performance with his Mark III during 1951. Nevertheless, there was only one of these made.

MARK V—There never was a Mark V Lotus, but there probably will be one someday when Chapman gets the time to design it. Piqued when the 750 Club declared his de-

The third Lotus ever built—the Mark III—is the extremely successful special that launched Chapman on a career of car building.

siamesing operation unconstitutional, he announced that he believed a 100-mph road sports car could be developed using an unsupercharged Austin-7 engine; Lotus Mark V was the designation reserved for it. He hasn't really tackled the problem yet, but gossip has it that his slide rule is leading him toward a plywood body.

MARK VI—This is the model that made the marque's name, although there were only about 100 kits sold. Designed so that it could be assembled with a minimum of tools by any talented amateur, the kit consisted of a Chapman-designed multi-tubular frame and modified Ford moving parts. Chapman, still working at British Aluminium, and his friend Michael Allen, chipped in to start Lotus Cars, Ltd. He hasn't divulged their capital, but it couldn't have been any spectacular amount, because as soon as they had built the prototype of the Mark VI the firm ran out of money. Fortunately, the prototype was demolished en route to a race in 1952, when it was only a month old, and the insurance payment put the business back on its feet.

Once in production, the Mark VI kits went like Fords, and eight of them were shipped before Chapman got a chance to put one together and try it out for himself.

MARK VII—This one he skipped.

MARK VIII—By 1952 Chapman realized that he could no longer attain top performance with conventional-bodied cars. The big drawback of a super-streamlined body is that it generally winds up weighing more than a plain, un-aerodynamic one. It took Chapman and Frank Costin, an aircraft engineer, 2 years to perfect the triangulated space frame and aerodynamic body for Mark VIII, but when they got through they had a really fast, scientifically streamlined vehicle. Powered by an engine made up of Morris 10 and TC MG bits and pieces, the low-drag body swept along so silently that Lotus mechs were involved in three crack-ups because they couldn't use wind-rush to judge their speed. Ten Mark VIIIs were built.

MARK IX—Basically a Mark VIII, with a few improvements. About forty were built in 1955. This year was a banner year for Lotus, for the marque's racing successes fill twelve legal-size pages, single spaced.

MARK X—1500-cc version of the Mark IX. About ten built.

MARK XI—This is the current Lotus, introduced in 1956, and it is the fanciest of them all. With a Coventry-Climax engine, disc brakes, and a deDion final drive it's called the Le Mans model; a live axle and drum brakes make it the Club model, and the same with a Ford 1172-cc engine is called the Sports model. Club and Le Mans models tack on a number after their name, depending on which Coventry-Climax engine they use. They are 75's if they are powered with the FWA 1098-cc engine with standard camshaft producing 74 bhp at 6250 rpm. The same engine with stage two camshaft (83 bhp at 6800 revs) makes the 85. The 90 gets its number from the FWE 1290-cc engine, for this delivers 91 bhp at 6500. An FWB 1460-cc mill

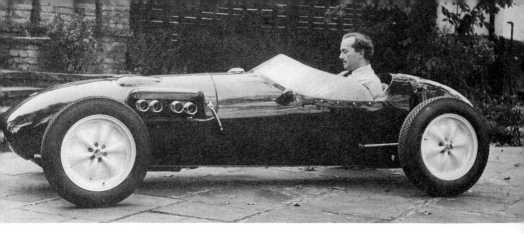

Colin Chapman in the Formula II Grand Prix Lotus racing car.

delivers 100 bhp at 6250, so it doesn't take an Einstein to figure out that this model will be the 100. And if daddy's rich, sonny gets a 140, equipped with the FPF twin overhead cam job, holding 1475 cubical centimeters and disgorging 141 bhp when you revolve it 7000 times in a minute.

The latest Lotus effort is Chapman's entry into the Gran Turismo market, the Lotus Elite, a pretty and potent little coupe that will bring the art of Lotus driving into the hands of those too faint of heart to enjoy the roadsters.

Close on the heels of the Mark XI, comes the F2, which marks Lotus's debut in formula racing. No matter how one figures Lotus production, it is hard to make the total of all models to add up to much over three hundred cars. Yet there are practically no sports or racing enthusiasts who haven't heard of the Lotus, and even fewer who haven't wanted one. This becomes all the more remarkable when one considers that Chapman spends next to nothing on advertising or publicity. The Lotus got its reputation when owners of the marque began talking it up, and held its reputation when competition laurels proved that the design had something. "If Colin were ever to build a mouse trap," said one driver, "I'd cerainly hate to be a mouse!"

The utter devotion that Chapman can inspire is a vital part of his organization. Many of his most valued co-workers are people whose main jobs are on some one else's payroll.

The aerodynamic body for the Mark VIII, for example, was subjected to exhaustive tests, including wind-tunnel routines and special rigs, using the facilities of an internationally famous aircraft firm. The firm can't be named, for this information would come as a surprise to them. Chapman just happened to have a friend on the staff. When Chapman noticed that the Coventry-Climax engine used in a fire pump would make an ideal lightweight power plant for a sports car, it required a lot of fast talking on his part to get the company to bother making the necessary modifications on such a small number of engines as he could order. In the course of his campaign, he completely won over Wally Hassan and Harry Munday, designers of the Fire Pump. Now Munday is his principal consultant on engines.

No matter how many volunteer helpers and well-wishers Chapman has, practically nothing about his future plans ever leaks out—for the simple reason that Chapman is a fanatic about keeping technical information secret. The Jelly Joint on the Mark II was hidden from view by a special aluminum plate, and he never loosened or tightened the bolts when there was a chance anyone could see. It took the 750 Club an entire season—during which Chapman cleaned up on trophies—before they wised up to the de-siamesed inlet ports on his Mark III. Coming more up-to-date, the first time anyone at Lotus Cars, Ltd., knew about the projected F2 was when the welders delivered a new frame. Of course, they all had an idea that there was something new cooking: Chapman hadn't been putting in as much time as usual at the plant. Such absences generally precede new developments, for he does designing at home.

When he departs from his usual secrecy, he always has a good reason. Associates were shocked, not long ago, when Chapman shipped two Mark VI kits to Maserati—for cash. "Next year Maserati will be producing Lotuses," they forecast.

"Nonsense," said Chapman. "First of all, they'll put

The current model Lotus with Chapman at the wheel.

Maserati engines in the Mark VI frames, and the frames will break. Our engines weigh 200 pounds; the Maseratis are close to 400. So they'll stiffen frames in the conventional way, and they'll be useless."

This is pretty much what happened. Chapman ended up with the profit on two kits, and Maserati ended up not much wiser than they were before. The following season, however, Lotuses began appearing powered by engines of essentially the same rating as the Maseratis, but weighing only the same 200 pounds the frame had been designed to take. Maserati had just tackled the wrong end of the problem; instead of stiffening the frame, they should have lightened the engine. Or, as they say in Kentucky: "Don't raise the levee, just lower the river!"

Colin's major weakness is one that could also be said to have been shared by the original Mr. Ford. His ability to take in money is accompanied by a parsimony that borders on miserliness in some ways. And, on occasion, Chapman has paid dearly for his nickel nursing. At least two instances have provided racing cognoscenti around the world with chuckles at his expense. When the Lotus Elites made their debut at the 1959 Sebring 12-hour endurance race, the rainfall set records. Chapman being Chapman had searched out the most inexpensive bottom in which to ship his cars. All might have been well for the four cars he shipped had it not been for two things. Somewhere in its travels the tramp steamer had picked up a load of grain which went into the hold *above* the Lotus equipe. On the ship's arrival in Miami some 3 days before the race, her skipper looked at the teeming sky and steadfastly refused to unbutton the hatches despite the importunate pleas of the Lotus team personnel. The master pointed out quite reasonably that he had picked up a load of grain and he was jolly well going to deliver a load of grain—not a load of porridge. The rain finally let up, and the cars just made shore in time for the race, with no time for practice or preparation.

Much the same thing happened later that year at the Grand Prix de Monaco, when a pair of Formula One cars were shipped off to the continent in a tired van equipped with a very small Ford engine. Somewhere in France the tired little engine no longer could. No parts were readily available, so new parts had to be flown in from England. It is not an uncommon occurrence to fly new racing parts about the world, but this was probably the first time a flight had to be made for an old truck. The cars arrived at the venue just in time for qualification runs. One didn't make it. The other one caught fire during the course of the race. For lack of a nail . . .

Chapman the driver, is a good deal like Chaliapin the singer: adequate but blood-curdling. Nobody is very surprised that he's prematurely grey, for the consensus is that if he had any nerves at all, he'd frighten himself into general paralysis every time he came up to the starting line. Described as a "press on, regardless" driver, it is rare for him to lift his foot off the accelerator during a race. Only his highly developed mechanical sympathy keeps him from blowing up engines, and only a benign providence keeps him alive long enough to collect the winner's garland. As an engineer, he maintains that any driver who spins off ought to be shot. As a driver he is constanly spinning off. But he hasn't shot himself yet.

His friends explain this very simply: there's no *money* in shooting yourself!

7. The Man From Modena
by Steve McNamara

It has been said that you could park a Ferrari in the middle of the Mojave desert and draw a crowd in ten minutes. The time element might be exaggerated but the statement, in the main, is true. Those automotive purists who say that the great men of motoring—those ducal builders who built for themselves alone—passed on with Ettore Bugatti reckon without the dedicated Modenese, Commendatore Enzo Ferrari. This strange, lonely man has seen the ideas of his fertile mind become the most successful series of competition cars of his day. At first chunky, squat, and brutal looking, now low and sleek, the cars of Enzo Ferrari have, in one short decade won almost every major race in the world. And those laurels that haven't been won by cars bearing the yellow shield with the black, prancing horse represent to Ferrari goals that *must* be attained. Dictatorial always, aloof and yet volatile, Ferrari is a fitting successor to the revered Bugatti, although in many ways he is an entirely different sort of man. Where

Bugatti was always the sculptor and artist, his designs light and airy, Ferrari is always the engineer; his cars show the rugged strength he demands. Where Bugatti would run off a completely different or new model almost at a whim, Ferrari sticks by what is proven and tried. Both men, however, have produced an amazing variety of different designs. It is said that only once in a generation does such a genius appear. This generation belongs to the man from Modena. He has no living equal.

Ferrari is a common name in Italy. It adorns countless bars and shoe stores and occupies that thick section in Italian telephone books which Jones or Smith do in the United States. But within the past 20 years the world has come to know Ferrari as the name of an extraordinary Italian whose crest— a black horse rampant on a yellow field—adorns the most successful racing cars in history.

Enzo Ferrari's comparatively heavy and incredibly tough cars have been in the public eye since, as Ferrari describes it, "I picked up the torch laid down by Alfa Romeo in 1937." Ferrari himself has remained remote. He is content to have his laurels shipped to Modena, and he steps forward only when pressured to do so.

This insistence on privacy has had predictable results: Admirers and detractors have woven stories around him composed of rumor and hearsay. In real life Ferrari is essentially a plain person of monumental will and dignity who, like his cars, is sturdy and powerful. The storytellers have found some grist for their gossip mills in the fact that Ferrari's life is full of paradoxes. It is most striking that, despite a fervent desire to lead a simple life, he has found himself in constant complications.

The red racing cars of Scuderia Ferrari have won more prize money than those of any other marque in history, yet Ferrari is not a rich man and the finances of his factory have

Enzo Ferrari, the man from Modena.

often been shaky. Ferrari has immense pride and awareness of his high position, yet he has been forced to make a public appeal for support. He dislikes arguments and bickering, yet he is involved in almost constant skirmishing with the Italian government and press, race organizers, suppliers, and customers. He is a former driver of considerable skill whose whole being is bound up tightly with his racing cars, yet for business and personal reasons he believes he should never be present when his cars are raced. He speaks earnestly of the "equally valuable lessons learned in defeat and victory," yet the pressure to win which surrounds his equipe is almost overpowering. Ferrari is one of the few men to obtain some measure of financial success by building competition cars, yet he believes himself hounded by disappointment and tragedy.

There is an Italian proverb that runs, "Donne e Motori, Gioie e Dolorie (Women and Engines, Delight and Anguish)." One of Ferrari's admirers once said that, as far as the engine end is concerned, there is no man to whom this proverb better applies than Enzo Ferrari.

Ferrari's beginnings were in no way extraordinary; no comet creased the sky when he was born more than 60 years ago in Modena, a farming and light-industry center of some 100,000 population situated in Emilia, a flat region in North-central Italy which lies within view of the mountains along the western coast of the Gulf of Genoa.

Modena is a pleasant, sunny, and unimposing city whose principal nonautomotive tourist attractions are a very old church, the Italian military academy, a local wine which tastes much like sparkling burgundy and, since Mussolini, a mammoth swimming pool. Like many Italian cities, it is fiercely provincial; when speaking among themselves the Modenese use a language which is quite remote from Italian and which they insist is the *lingua madre* of all Italy. A friend defended Ferrari's refusal to learn English by remarking that he already speaks three languages: Italian, French, and Modenese.

Enzo Ferrari's father owned a small ironworks in Modena (the name Ferrari, itself, is a derivative of the Italian word for iron.) His father's business nurtured Enzo's predeliction for automobiles since, along with bicycle repair shops, ironworks were hotbeds of early automotive interest. Ferrari says, "Henry Ford was the man responsible for the dreams of my youth." Apparently the tinkering and the dreams took up too much time; young Ferrari did not do at all well in technical school.

When Ferrari was eighteen his father was killed in World War I. His mother had died earlier and when, shortly after his father's death, Ferrari's older brother died, it meant the end of the family business. This was the beginning of a string of personal sorrows which are a strong reason for Ferrari's desire for a secluded life.

Ferrari moved to Turin and went to work in *Costruzioni Meccaniche Nazionale* (later the Piaggio scooter company). There followed a long period of only modest progress along the automotive path. Once he got his "break," however, progress was swift. In 1932 he began racing a modified Alfa, and a year later he joined the Alfa factory team. He was a skillful driver, but gained only modest success. In an era when only favored few commanded anything like a living wage, Ferrari's wallet was often very lean.

After 2 years as a team driver, he became Alfa's racing manager in 1935. His 4-year term was no picnic; Alfa was faced with Germany's silver meteors. Hitler-prodded and state-assisted, Mercedes-Benz and Auto Union were invincible . . . they put out Alfa's torch. Ferrari grew to have little warmth for the Germans, a feeling which later events would increase.

Those 4 years also had their more rewarding aspects. In addition to his managerial duties Ferrari was named the Alfa agent for Modena and Emilia's adjoining provinces. The money began trickling in, and Ferrari was able to open repair shops in Modena and on farm property owned by the family 10 miles southeast of Modena and on the outskirts of the village of Maranello.

By 1939 he felt sufficiently well fixed to buy some Alfas and start his own *scuderia*. He was to pioneer many aspects of racing-team management; Ferrari was the first to form a private team, a concept taken up in the United States on varying scales by Briggs Cunningham, John Edgar, Temple Buell, and George Tilp, and most successfully in Great Britain by Rob Walker.

It was also in 1939 that Ferrari became a *Commendatore*, a title he wears with great dignity and which is used scrupulously by all his associates when they address him. This puzzles some people because in recent years *Commendatore* has become a not overly impressive title which its owners usually pack away for formal occasions. The explanation is that Ferrari was the first man who worked with his hands to be so honored and, at the time the award was made, there were only 125 living *Commendatores*. Ferrari attaches considerably more importance to it than to the nominally more important *Cavaliere del Lavoro*, which he was awarded in 1954. In addition, his first award was bestowed by King Victor Emanuel III, and Ferrari's political sympathies are more with the good old days than with the republic, which on occasion has criticized him so severely.

After establishing his shop in Modena, Ferrari set about making his cars more Ferrari than Alfa. In 1940 the first Ferrari to ever race, an 8-cylinder, 1500-cc model, won a closed-circuit event near Modena. The driver was Alberto Ascari, the man who in later years was almost as much of an asset to the team as Ferrari himself.

Ferrari and Ascari had time for but a few more races before the war. Ferrari converted his Modena shop into a machine-tool factory. He did quite well, and his ledger showed a nice profit until the Americans bombed the plant. In Ferrari's view this was a war risk, but what happened next rankled him a great deal. The Germans rolled up to the factory, cleared away some of the rubble, loaded what was left of the machinery

General view of the tools department at the Farrari factory in Modena.

on trucks, and drove away. He was totally defeated in persistent attempts to exact payment for the machinery from what were supposed to be his allies. Ferrari gathered together what was left in the factory and moved his operations to the repair shop outside Maranello, a location which he hoped to be more isolated from both American planes and plundering Germans.

The Maranello factory has been expanded year by year until today, on the inside, it is a quite modern plant employing about three hundred men in both the racing and GT divisions. With the exception of the imposing dark-red-brick front with high fencing, the outside still looks more like a farm than a factory. It is a modest, low, rambling structure plumped down amidst poplar and mulberry trees supporting grape vines. The racing and GT divisions are separated by an informal courtyard which serves as a storage area for raw material. The poplar-lined road to Modena is used to test the GT's; drivers try to arrange the higher speed runs around lunch time or whenever traffic is thin.

Maserati and Stanguellini build cars in Modena and Scaglietti builds bodies, but Ferrari builds nothing whatsoever there. The Modena building serves for the servicing of customers' GT's, the offices of *Ferrari Automobili* and, atop the offices, the small apartment in which Ferrari and his wife live. There are also Ferrari service centers in Rome, Milan, and Turin, but most Italian customers perfer to bring their cars to Modena.

After the war, Ferrari began to rebuild. Through his vast technical experience and, above all, his determination and will power, Ferrari racing cars became more and more respected and feared.

By 1952 Ferrari had reached a position of dominance. Alberto Ascari's years of toil paid off with the first of his two straight world championships. In the next six seasons Ferrari won five sports-car titles and Ferrari drivers won the championship three times. The three years a Ferrari driver did not win (1954, 1955, 1957) Fangio was responsible. In 1956 somebody announced after long study that Ferrari cars had won 503 races in 9 years. Of course, he couldn't even begin to tote up the hundreds of small-race results, and Ferrari victories, that never make the record books. Since then, nobody has tried seriously to count Ferrari wins.

The year 1952 also marked the first of Ferrari's two frustrating encounters with the Indianapolis Motor Speedway. Four cars were sent to Indiana with guarded hopes of victory since, after all, it hadn't been so long since Wilbur Shaw had mopped up with a Maserati. It turned out to have been long enough for the construction of Indianapolis cars to have developed into a highly specialized art, quite apart from the construction of Grand Prix or sports cars. Three of the Ferraris failed to qualify and the fourth, driven by Ascari, cracked up early in the race. Ferrari tried again in 1956 with Nino Farina at the wheel, but the results were no better. Ferrari was sorely disappointed and not a little humiliated. When questioned each year since about the possibility of entering, he has disclaimed interest. But those who know the *Commendatore* find it difficult to believe that he has written off the Brickyard.

In the 1952 Indianapolis affair there were several sprinkles of disappointment, but 1955 was the year of the great deluge. After years of planning, Mercedes-Benz again unleashed its silver cars. With Mercedes able to call on the talents of Fangio and Moss and on its virtually unlimited financial and technical resources, Ferrari found the struggle even more unequal than during his prewar years with Alfa. Mercedes flashed home first in race after race; with Stirling Moss aboard, a Mercedes set the record which still stands for the Mille Miglia, until then almost a Ferrari fief.

The loss of the Mille Miglia was insignificant compared to the loss of Ascari, who died at Monza testing the car of his protegé, Eugenio Castelotti. Ascari, whose effortless style surpassed even that of Fangio, had been a mainstay of *Scuderia Ferrari* in lean years and fat. The shock of his death was increased by the almost mystic similarity between its circumstances and those surrounding the test-drive death of Ascari's father.

Right on the heels of Ascari's death the Pirelli bomb was dropped. Before and since Ferrari has had squabbles with his suppliers, most notably with the body makers who object to Ferrari taking a cut of their price to the customer. All these troubles pale when compared to the Pirelli epic.

Early one week Pirelli announced that it was no longer giving the usual 12 to 25 per cent racing discount on its tires: starting immediately, all purchasers, including *Scuderia Ferrari,* must pay the retail price. This was a serious blow to the

Ferrari financial structure; in order to survive without the subsidies of a huge production-car division or a private fortune, Ferrari had come to depend on contracts with suppliers. Two recent examples show how important he considers these contracts: tests at Silverstone in 1958 showed the new Dunlops to be quite superior to Engleberts, but Ferrari refused to switch until the Englebert contract had run out. Last March at Sebring Ferrari flatly refused to race unless his Shell contract could be observed.

Under the circumstances it is hardly surprising that Ferrari lost his temper with Pirelli. Adding to his anger, and probably a factor in Pirelli's decision, was the fact that the tires had been giving trouble. One had blown out on Count Marzotto's Mille Miglia car, nearly causing a serious crash, and a few miles up the road in the same race a tire on Castelotti's car had lost a tread.

Ferrari fired off an announcement that never again would he use Pirelli tires. Then he turned around to face the prospect of racing his cars on the rims. Mercedes had an iron grip on Continental, and had no intention of supplying its chief rival with superior rubber. At that time Dunlop's nationalistic fervor was stronger than its sales department, and the firm declined to have its tires used against British cars. Michelin felt approximately the same way, and it was too late to set up a contract with an American firm. With a race to be driven the next weekend, Ferrari turned to, of all persons for an Italian to ask for assistance, a woman.

Belgium was one of the few European countries which had not thrown up a tariff wall in front of Ferrari's GT's, and the Princess of Rhety had become one of his best customers. Ferrari made his plight known to the Princess; by nightfall Engleberts were on their way to Maranello. Ferrari's dark mood concerning Pirelli turned even blacker when Englebert made great publicity of the fact that Ferrari was racing on Belgian tires. Ferrari is a great waver of the Italian flag, and he bitterly regretted being forced by an Italian firm to go outside the country for any of his main supplies.

When the season ended Ferrari had won ninety-three races all over the world, but ninety-two of them were minor events and of no financial help to the factory. Only one major race had been won by a Ferrari: The Grand Prix of Monaco (ironically, that was the last time a Ferrari had won there).

On the subject of victory and defeat Ferrari can speak in a very philosophical vein: "When I enter a race I do not think of my competitors. I don't say to myself, 'I must beat Mercedes or Maserati.' It is the technical result of a race that counts." The technical results of the 1955 season were apparently very bad; or, and more to the point, Ferrari hates to lose, literally cannot afford to lose because prize money pays a large part of *Scuderia Ferrari's* expenses. At the close of the season Ferrari shook his organization from bottom to top. Racing Manager Nello Ugolini was given his walking papers (he walked into Maserati and took the comparable job); Maserati's chief engineer, Vittorio Bellenta, was hired; all team drivers with the exception of Castelotti were fired; Fangio was picked up from Mercedes; free-lancer Peter Collins was signed, and another attempt was made to add Moss.

This brightened the prospects for 1956, but it had no effect on the empty cash register. Ferrari swallowed his great pride and made a public appeal for support. "It is Italian engineering and artisanship that wins on the track when Ferraris win," he said. "I have problems which the Germans do not have. While for them their cars are representative of the nation and the maker benefits from their help and cooperation, I often have to worry about how to meet my men's wages. Workers and Italian emigrants send me letters of appreciation and congratulation from all over the world. That is most comforting." But, Ferrari went on, that wasn't paying the bills.

He definitely was not looking for help from the government. As he said later, "It is good that we have no government subsidy. If we had the state as a master, then where would we be? It is better to have no master and to rely on oneself." At that dark hour in 1955 Ferrari was relying on the sympathy and generosity of Italian industry.

The response on the whole was a shattering silence. Most Italian industrialists felt they had no more business supporting Ferrari than he had boosting their motor scooters, shoes, or movies. However, Lancia turned over all its racing cars (ostensibly of dubious value since they had won but one race all season) and Fiat contributed 50 million lire (80 thousand dollars). Fiat's 50 million perhaps meant the difference between life and death for Ferrari Automobili; and it is no coincidence that Ferrari's personal car is a Fiat 1200 coupe and all Ferraris travel in Fiat transporters.

Thanks to the 50 million lire and the revamped Lancias, 1956 saw Ferrari firmly in the win column again. The most comforting victory was the incredibile quintuple in the Mille Miglia, a record not likely to be equaled in any motor race. But Ferrari's return to racing triumph was overshadowed by a personal tragedy. Ferrari's 28-year-old son Dino, his hope for the creation of a dynasty, died in late June. Even taking into account the traditional love of the Italian for his children, Ferrari was very devoted to this, his only son. Dino's death was a terrible blow and, added to the fact of his wife's frequent illnesses, it greatly increased Ferrari's natural inclination to stay near home.

When I asked Ferrari to name his greatest disappointment in racing he replied, "There have been so many, too many, and I could not single out one. I feel lost against the cruelty of destiny." The 1957 season contained two of these racing sorrows. Almost before the season had begun Castelotti died in a car intended for Sebring, the second Italian driver to die at Monza testing a Ferrari. Sebring and victory passed, and it was time for the Mille Miglia.

The Mille Miglia was Ferrari's favorite race. As a young man he had followed it passionately as the cars hurtled through Modena, and later he had raced its grueling length himself. "The Mille Miglia costs nothing to look at. It is the race of the people," he said before the 1957 race. "One may say that the whole of Italy leans forward with her eyes on the tarred strip of road somewhere along the course on Mille Miglia Day. It is a day when I feel my life is useful, that I am accomplishing something." Toward the end of that day a Ferrari driven by the Marquis de Portago rocketed off the road into a ditch and burned, killing Portago, his companion, Edward Nelson, and 10 spectators.

Long before the race there had been rumblings in the Italian Parliament and press about abolition of the event. In virtually every running of the race at least one driver or spectator had been killed or injured. Portago's crash resulted in even greater publicity than the great Le Mans disaster of 1955. Portago was one of the era's most romantic figures and made great newspaper copy; there was even something for the movie magazines, because Fon's most recent conquest was supposed to have been Linda Christian.

Italy's Parliament and press opened up with both barrels. A successful bill to outlaw the race was whipped into shape, and Ferrari was attacked with great vigor. All his Mille Miglia car were impounded by the government, with accompanying hints that they were mechanically faulty.

Although extremely sensitive to press criticism, Ferrari has always refused to be drawn into polemics with his critics, critics whose harshness would surprise Americans who consider him to be almost sacrosanct in his own country. But nearly 2 months after the Portago crash, when officials were still trying to find something wrong with his cars (they never did), Ferrari jolted the racing world by withdrawing his cars from the Grand Prix of Italy at Monza. This set off new press attacks; Ferrari replied that "We shall never again race in

Italy." Along with Ferrari brakes and suspension the officials had been examining Englebert tires. In a statement supporting Ferrari's "withdrawal," Englebert said that in view of the impossible atmosphere created by Italian authorities, they would supply no more tires for Italian cars in Italian races.

But the very next season, 1958, Ferrari automobiles were racing in Italy and racing on Englebert tires. The Englebert explanation was simple: Their statement had been made at Ferrari's prodding, and if the *Commendatore* had changed his mind, then Englebert would be only too happy to supply the tires.

A man's mind is his private domain, and Enzo Ferrari is not given to making excuses or explanations. But it will help to understand this incident, and an exactly similar one a year later, if one remembers that Ferrari is not an American; he is an Italian, and Italians have different ways of doing things than their less-spirited neighbors to the north. An example is an Italian strike. American bus drivers or auto workers walk off the job, march up and down in front of the plant with signs, and don't go back to work until they get their raise or get very hungry. Italian bus drivers and auto workers make ringing declarations to the press about the dire need for a raise, march home, sit around drinking or fishing for a day, and go back to work the next day. In the area below Switzerland the *gesture* is of considerable importance.

For both triumphs and tragedies, 1958 was better and worse than 1957. Mike Hawthorn became Ferrari's fourth yearly world champion and Ferrari won its sixth sports-car championship in a runaway. And Luigi Musso and Peter Collins died driving Ferraris, in accidents of such a nature that even Ferrari's defenders wondered if perhaps there wasn't something inherently unsafe about his cars.

Ascari's death had been so spooky—he apparently had lost control on a straightaway at a fairly slow speed—that it seemed, in a way, divorced from normal experience. Castelotti, an

The Ferrari team at Neuburgens, 1952.

erratic driver, was supposed to have crashed as a result of his
own flagrant error—missing a downshift. In the 1957 tragedy,
Portago probably blew a tire which was bald of his own choosing. But both Musso and Collins died driving cars in normal
condition through high-speed bends they had taken many
times before. There was a chance Musso had been groggy
from nitro fumes gulped at the Monza "500" a week before,
but this is rather far-fetched.

Some said Ferraris had been so perfected that drivers lost

the natural feel of the car and were apt to overestimate its capacities. Others said that, although the FI cars were smaller, lighter, had less cylinder capacity and power, and handled better than the cars of 10 years ago, the drivers were more reckless, trusted their cars more, and took curves at too-high speeds. Still others claimed that Fangio was at fault: drivers were trying to drift high-speed bends as he had done, even though none had his superhuman judgment.

The Italian press was in full howl. It went so far as to charge Ferrari with building death traps which were wiping out the world's best drivers and, more criminal yet, had killed *every one* of Italy's first rank drivers.

Ferrari replied, in a rare press conference, that "After the tragic incidents in regard to which the Italian press has inflicted grave moral condemnation on us, we asked ourselves, together with our technicians, if we had actually overlooked something that might have caused disasters. But we came to the conclusion that we had done everything humanly and technically possible to prevent and avoid any incident whatsoever. There was a time in Italy when races were highly exalted, then merely tolerated. Today they are virtually on the Index. I no longer feel at my age like continuing such a battle. That is why I say we will no longer race in Italy." (Ferrari raced in Italy the very next season.)

Why all the deaths? Ferrari himself blames the circuits, charging in particular that retaining bankings have not been modified to cope with higher racing speeds. But the fact remains that the death toll of *Scuderia Ferrari* is higher than for any other equipe. Whether today's FI cars, and Ferrari's FI cars in particular, are inherently unsafe is a question which seems impossible to answer.

But in all the wild polemics one fact seems to have been overlooked: race driving, especially highly competitive race driving, is a dangerous occupation; death is an occupational hazard. *Scuderia Ferrari* hires the most competitive drivers;

as Ferrari says, "The results of a race are only due 50 per cent to the car. When you have created a car that can win you have only come half way. The moment has come to find a driver." Even in the select world of GP drivers there are many "strokers" who never take big chances, never win many races, and live to a ripe old age. A very few drivers have the ability to drive very quickly without taking big chances. Fangio is the outstanding example and Tony Brooks the best active one. In the main it is the "chargers" who finish near the top by taking sometimes-fatal chances. *Scuderia Ferrari*, which must win, has employed more than its share of "chargers," and consequently has had more than its share of deaths.

Although most certainly aware of thepressure to win, Ferrari drivers in general have pleasant relations with the *Commendatore*. He seems to understand them and their way of life; as he puts it, "It is easier to interpret a part of life when you have lived the same part, whether for passion or for necessity." However, the drivers definitely feel they are employees, not collaborators. There is no togetherness in Modena, and the ties between drivers are purely personal friendships.

Ferrari's attitude toward test driving and actual racing acknowledges the pressure that exists. His daily routine usually consists of working at the Modena office until 3 P.M., when a combination chauffeur-office guard drives him to Maranello where he stays until 7. Quite often he spends the late morning at Modena's combination airport-auto circuit taking a commanding interest in tests. (He occasionally tests a GT himself, but never a GP or sports car.) He believes he must supervise the testing, but, as noted before, it is virtually front-page news when he appears at a race.

He says, "I suffer badly when I see one of my cars not go as well as it should or when a driver risks himself too much. It seems obvious that my presence would cause embarrassment to the drivers and mechanics." His men are acutely

aware that Racing Manager Romulo Tavoni has detailed telephone or cable communications with Ferrari at the conclusion
of practice sessions and the race, but that's not the same as
having the *Commendatore* sitting on the pit wall.

Ferrari has another professional reason for staying at
home which might seem a trifle strange to those who think
only of *Scuderia Ferrari* and forget about *Ferrari Automobili*.
He doesn't junket around the world with his cars, as does
Briggs Cunningham, Ferrari·says, "because I consider my daily
work useful and necessary for the life of my firm *(Ferrari
Automobili).* I have very good collaborators who can handle
the racing *(Scuderia Ferrari).* My presence is much more important at the firm."

The 350 GT's that *Ferrari Automobili* turns out in a
year are not prestige-publicity items such as David Brown's
Aston-Martin GT's; they occupy a crucial spot on the balance
sheet. While Brown can charge off his GT and racing losses
to his gear-box and tractor empire, Ferrari must not only
make money on his GT's, but in lean racing years this profit
has had to help support *Scuderia Ferrari*.

Ferrari's delicate financial balance has not endeared him
to some customers and race organizers. The price of a GT,
especially in Europe, can vary considerably. It's not unusual
for a customer's wallet to be assayed and expensive accessories
added accordingly. One Roman prince is reported to have
found a gilded steering wheel on his car—and paid for it.

The American market is a lucrative one for Ferrari, but
it has its problems. Ferrari says the *raison d'être* of *Scuderia
Ferrari* is "to build cars for champions to win championships
in." He would like to carry this princely approach over into
the GT division, and in Europe he has been fairly successful,
picking and choosing his customers. But the greater pool of
Ferrari-type money is in the United States, and the necessity
to tap it has meant that a number of Ferraris have found their
way into the hands of people who do not measure up to the

A 4.9 Ferrari driven by test driver Enrique Valiente.

Commendatore's driving and breeding standards. These persons, failing to understand their good fortune in being allowed to buy a Ferrari, have expected the same kind of service they get with a Chevrolet or a Renault and have gone so far as to complain that the plugs foul at low speeds. (The latter problem is aggravated by the fact that some purchasers take the high-speed axle to impress their friends and then drive the car almost exclusively at low speeds.)

The GT division can be made to produce a profit, but nothing like the Porsche, Jaguar, or Mercedes earnings. As Ferrari explains it, "The expenses of yearly racing cannot be charged off to the rest of the firm because it is a small firm. The racing expenses must be paid for with starting money, prize money, and help from the accessory suppliers." Nobody is more aware of this situation than the race organizers. Ferrari pioneered the practice of starting money, and he practices it relentlessly. One organizer, after several years of dealing with Ferrari's demands, came to the disgruntled conclusion that Ferrari considers himself the Pope of motor racing.

There is no doubt that Ferrari is, and considers himself, one of the great figures of automotive history. He refers to himself in the grand manner; he is likely to say "Ferrari believes that . . ." rather than "I believe that . . ." There is a great deal of the automotive statesman in his bearing. He is much too experienced a hand to be trapped in the Fangio vs. Nuvolari wrangle: His response to a "who was the greater driver?" question was, "Every period has had the greatest driver. Sportsmen, like politicians, cannot be judged apart from the time in which they lived."

Ferrari also refuses to be drawn into an argument over Stirling Moss, who says he will not drive for Ferrari because all the good drivers should not drive for one team and he (Moss) was slighted by Ferrari years ago. When told of Moss' position, Ferrari replied with heavy irony that "For a long time I have considered Moss one of the greatest *'fighter-drivers'* in the world. The reasons for which he declares he will not drive for Ferrari represent his personal truth. But as the truth is a very subjective thing, it is obvious that all of us indulge ourselves in building our own 'truth'."

Ferrari is in many ways austere and remote in his approach to his customers. The Ferrari manner bears a striking resemblance to that of Ettore Bugatti. In the way of *Le Patron,* the *Commendatore* exercises complete control over his factory, indeed, he IS the factory. He weighs the advice of his associates, but he is *Ferrari*—all decisions of any importance are his personal province. Many an axle ratio has been changed on the eve of a race after a cabled command from Modena. It would be wrong to say that he rules with an iron hand; his iron will is quite sufficient.

Ferrari ascribes his success to "the result of a common effort of men who believed in me and worked with dedication." Despite little or no public credit, these men are fanatically loyal. One Ferrari critic says that this is simply because there is nowhere else for them to work, but this theory skirts the tremendous respect, if not affection, which Ferrari commands.

Bugatti is the principal challenger to Ferrari's title of the only man to make a financial success of automobiles based on speed. However, *Le Patron* occasionally turned out an opulent creation that had little to do with quickness. Bugatti also differed widely from Ferrari in development and testing procedures. Bugatti was fond of new ideas; after creating a new rear suspension he would place it on two sawhorses and have six men stand on it to see if it was sturdy enough.

Ferrari is not fond of new ideas; he only switched to disc brakes years after they were proved superior to the drum variety for racing purposes. His new cars are invariably too heavy, and he makes them go faster by subtracting weight only after exhaustive tests have convinced him that the subtracted components won't affect the car's durability. This cautious approach, plus Ferrari's fixation with metal fatigue (something Bugatti never heard of), have resulted in Ferrari's present reputation for durability. This reputation was not always so; clutch and starter on past Ferraris have given great trouble. His solution was the predictable one involving the addition of weight.

Ferrari views metal fatigue with a horror akin to a driver's attitude toward oil on the course. He fights it with a small but highly knowledgable engineering department in a very modern laboratory, and in test after test on Modena's oval track. The results caused one Briton, not an admirer, to remark, "Once a Ferrari leaves Modena it's ready. If a driver bashes it one Sunday, a mechanic hammers it out and it's ready by next Sunday. Our cars often must be flown home. Once a Ferrari leaves the works it can generally be sorted out by a mechanic."

Ferrari is explicit in indicating that he spends little time contemplating past triumphs: "It is human nature to discount your past achievements and look forward to new ones, to feel the past achievements will be insignificant compared to what will come." And he is serious in his views that each race is another test: "Motor races were, are, and always will be a spectacle with high technical meaning. They are proofs in practice of technical principles which could never be reproduced in a laboratory."

If each race is a test, what is he testing for? Ferrari's ambition, he says, is "to win the races that have never been won by Ferrari . . . and those races that have not been run."

There are but a handful of current races that Ferrari has not won. Two are quickly apparent: The Nurburgring and Indianapolis. A victory at the Nurburgring would be especially sweet if it came over a strong German threat. It would help ease those memories of the '30s, '40s, and '50s. The Indianapolis "500" failures would to a great extent be absolved by a victory in the proposed 3.8-liter Intercontinental Formula race there. The scheduled Sebring FI race is a logical target.

During his "withdrawal" press conference in 1958 Ferrari hinted strongly that he would soon give up motor racing. When asked later if he had any plans concerning the 1.5-liter FI ruling, he said simply, "Ferrari will be ready." From this extraordinary Italian with the ordinary name, the latter pronouncement seems suitable for all occasions.

Part III

THE RACERS:
Brains, Hands, and a Good Right Foot

Motor racing is more than a sport, it is a way of life, and the men who live it are a very special breed. Invariably, they love the life they lead, though they don't all love the cars they drive. Racing is not something a man can take up and put aside, as he would a harlot; rather, it is like a wild and loving mistress. It gets in the blood, and once there it stays.

Now, it is not merely a matter of getting into a fast car and pushing the throttle to the floor. As Denis Jenkinson points out in his thoughtful *The Racing Driver,* not everyone who drives a car in competition can be considered a racing driver. There are some who compete in small club events who fit the term, and there are others who drive in international events who never will become real racing drivers. And if anyone is qualified to make that statement, it is probably Jenkinson, who has seen more drivers at close range than any other living man not himself a racer.

Nor are all racers alike. Each is in himself a different individual, sharing only that peculiar combination of nerve, muscle, and skill that alone can make the difference that separates the motor-vehicle operator from the driver.

We invite you now to meet seven such men, men to whom a car is or was something more than a vehicle to transport a human body from point to point, men for whom a car could come alive.

8. The Man Who Could Do Everything
by Ken Purdy

Ken Purdy claims that his favorite occupation after collecting Bugattis is that of collecting people. It is extremely doubtful if the redoubtable Purdy will ever again collect such a prize as the Marquis de Portago. For that matter, it is just as doubtful that anyone now living will ever find such a person, for men such as this seldom appear more than once in a century.

Strictly speaking, de Portago was not just a racing man—he was a sportsman in the broad, if not the purest, sense of the word. Swordsman, horseman, flyer, Portago was one of those very few men blessed with the rare physical make-up with which he could do virtually anything he set his mind to—and do it better than most men.

But more than being a mere physical and neurological specimen, Alfonso de Portago was a human being. In the following word portrait, author Purdy has cut through the outward aura of glamor that surrounded the man in order to get at the man himself. Not a mere listing of deeds and misdeeds, this is the story of Portago as few other know him.

Don Alfonso Cabeza de Vaca y Leighton, Carvajal y Are, Conde de la Mejorada, Marquis de Portago, was 28 when he died at Guidizzollo, a few miles from Brescia and the end of the Mille Miglia, on the 12th of May, 1957. Portago had been a flier, jai-alai player, poloist, steeplechase rider (the world's leading amateur in 1951 and 1952), Olympic bobsledder and record-holder, remarkable swimmer, and he was, at his death, one of the dozen best racing drivers in the world.

He had never sat in a racing car until 1954, but he believed he would be champion of the world before 1960—and most of the men he ran against every week thought that he very well might be. If he lived.

Certainly, Portago was uniquely gifted. An athlete all his life, he was not a big man, not heavily muscled, but he had unusual strength, great endurance, abnormal eyesight, and a quickness of reaction that was legendary among his friends. He was highly intelligent, courteous, and very much aware of the world around him.

Gregor Grant, editor of the British weekly *Autosport,* said just before the Mille Miglia, "A man like Portago appears only once in a generation, and it would probably be more accurate to say only once in a lifetime. The fellow does *everything* fabulously well. Never mind the driving, the steeplechasing, the bobsledding, and the athletic side of things. Never mind the being fluent in four languages. There are so many other aspects to the man: for example, I think he could be the best bridge player in the world if he cared to try; he could certainly be a great soldier; and I suspect he could be a fine writer."

Portago's death, I suppose, proved again the two old British aphorisms: "Motor racing is a sport at which you get better and better until you get killed" and the other, less optimistic, "There are two kinds of racing drivers: those who get killed before they get good, and those who get killed afterward." But whether they die at the wheel sooner or later or not at all, most men have to serve years of apprenticeship before they make the big leagues: the racing team of one of the major factories. They drive sports cars, stock and not-so-stock, in rallies and dreary airport events; they cadge rides in scruffy hand-me-down racing cars, hoping to attract a wealthy sponsor's eye. When—and if—they are invited to Italy or Germany or France or England to sign a racing contract, they have behind them thousands of miles of competitive driving in dozens

Portago with Champion of the World, Juan Manuel Fangio, at the French Grand Prix.

of makes of cars. This is standard, this is usual, and, as with most of the other rules, Portago was the exception. Driving relief in his first race, the 1,000 kilometers for sports cars at Buenos Aires in 1954, he did three laps so badly that he dropped the car from second place to fifth—because he had never learned how to shift gears! To the day he died he had driven few makes of competition automobiles: Maserati, Osca, Ferrari. He never drove the usual sports cars, MG's, Jaguars, and so on. For personal use—before he began to compete, he usually drove American cars: Fords, something else that may have been a DeSoto, he wasn't sure. Explaining this, the last time I talked with him, he said, "Automobiles bore me, I know next to nothing about them, and I care less.

"I have no sentimental attachment for a car," he said. "I

can hardly tell one from another. Sometimes I make a little scratch in a car, in an inconspicuous place, so I can recognize it the next time I'm in it, so I can remember its defects. I'm not interested in cars. To me they're a means of transportation, or a machine for racing.

"When I have a racing car that I'm going to drive, I walk up to it, and I look at it, and I think, 'Now, is this son-of-a-bitch going to hold together for the next 500 kilometers?' That's the only interest I have in it. And as soon as the race is over, I couldn't care less what happens to it.

"I think some drivers are not only indifferent to their cars, but hostile to them. They look at the car before a race and they think, 'Now, what is this thing going to do to me today —how is it going to let me down, or make me lose the race— or perhaps even kill me?'"

Portago's forthright disclaimer of interest in the machines on which his career was based was typical. To the outermost limits which custom and law allowed, the 12th Marquis de Portago said precisely that he pleased and did exactly what he liked. When he saw a girl friend in the crowd lining the streets at the Rome check point in his last race, he stood on the brakes, locked everything up, waited for her, kissed her, and held her in his arms until an official furiously waved him on. The girl, of course, was Linda Christian, and Portago was probably the only man in the race who would have allowed himself such a gesture—at the risk of his life. Portago was an avowed romantic, and he had remarked that in another age he would have been a Crusader, or a knight-errant. He often dressed in black; his hair was black and curly, usually long over his neck and ears, clinging to his head like a skullcap; he moved quickly and rarely smiled; he sometimes looked like a juvenile delinquent or a hired killer; but more often like what he was, a Spanish grandee. The remark that he had been born 3 or 4 centuries too late was a cliche among his friends.

"Every time I look at Fon," one of them said, "I see him

in a long black cape, a sword sticking out of it, a floppy black hat on his head, riding like a fiend across some castle drawbridge."

When he began to drive Portago was not the best-loved figure on the international circuit—nor was he when he died, if it comes to that. Lacking the technical skill to balance his bitterly competitive instinct, he was dangerous in his first races, and to most people he seemed arrogant and supercilious. He was reputed to be enormously wealthy, he was a great lady-killer, and if he was not pugnacious, still, he was quick to fight. Most of the other drivers preferred to leave him alone. Nobody expected him to be around for very long in any case. Many thought he was just another aristocratic dilettante who would quickly lose interest in racing cars, but the few who knew his lineage were not so sure. His mother, an Englishwoman who brought a great fortune to his father, is a firm-minded woman; and a determined lust for adventure, plus an inclination for government, runs through the Portago line. Spanish history is studded with the name. In the sixteenth century one of Portago's forbears, Cabeza de Vaca, was shipwrecked on the Florida coast. He *walked* to Mexico City, recruiting an army as he went. Another conquered the Canary Islands, another was a leader in the fight to drive the Moors out of Spain. Portago's grandfather was governor of Madrid. His father was Spain's best golfer, polo player, yachtsman; he was also a fabulous gambler, said to have once won $2 million at Monte Carlo; he was a soldier and a movie actor. He died of a heart attack on the polo field, playing against his doctor's orders. The last king of Spain, Alfonso XIII, was Portago's godfather and namesake.

Naturally enough, in the light of his background and his own propensity for high-risk sports, Portago was constantly accused of fearlessness, of clinging to a death wish, and whatnot. We talked at length about that, the last time I saw Portago. He sat in my room in the Kenilworth in Sebring.

Portago had been very punctual and had apologized for being unable to keep his promise that there would be no interruptions—he had placed a phone call to Caracas, and he asked if he might tell the operator to put it on my wire when it came through. I wanted to record the interview; would he object to a Minifon? He said he would not, and then told me about an interview recording he was making for Riverside Records, a house specializing in sports-car material. We talked generalities for half an hour, and then I turned the machine on. I mentioned a newspaper article that had said something to the effect that he "lived on fear."

"A lot of nonsense," Portago said. "I'm often frightened. I can get frightened crossing the street in heavy traffic. And I know I'm a moral coward. I can't even go into a shop to look around and walk out without buying something. As for enjoying fear, I don't think anybody enjoys fear, at least in my definition, which is a mental awareness of a danger to your body. You can enjoy courage—the performance of an act which frightens you—but not fear.

"I know that my first ride in a racing car frightened me. That was the Mexican road race in 1953. I had been riding horses in competition for a long time, at least twice a week for 2 years, but I had to give it up because I put on some weight I couldn't get rid of. I couldn't get by no matter what I tried, and I tried most things: weighing in with papier-mâche boots and saddle made to look like leather and weighing nothing, or hiding a 5-pound weight on the scale so that the whole standard of weight for all the riders would go up!

"I met Harry Schell and Luigi Chinetti at the Paris auto show in 1953, and Chinetti asked me to be his co-driver in the Pan American race. All he really wanted me for, of course, was ballast. I didn't drive a foot, not even from the garage to the starting line. I just sat there, white with fear, holding on to anything I thought looked sturdy enough. I knew that Chinetti was a very good driver, a specialist in long-distance

Portago at speed at Sebring in a Ferrari.

races who was known to be conservative and careful; but the first time you're in a racing car you can't tell if the driver is conservative or a wild man, and I didn't see how Chinetti could get away with half of what he was doing. We broke down the second day of the race, but I had decided by then that this was what I wanted to do more than anything else, so I bought a 3-liter Ferrari.

"I was fortunate, of course, in being able to buy my own car. I think it might have taken me 5 or 6 years longer to make the Ferrari team if I had had to look around for a sponsor and all that. I was lucky having enough money to buy my own car— even if I'm not 'enormously wealthy.' In those years I was perpetually in debt." (Portago had various trust funds, but his mother controlled the family fortune which was of American origin and reputed to be high in the millions. In his heyday as a driver, Portago earned perhaps $40,000 a year.)

Harry Schell and Portago took the 3-liter to the Argentine for the 1,000-kilometer sports-car race.

"Harry was so frightened that I would break the car he wouldn't teach me how to change gear, so when after 70 laps (the race was 101) he was tired and it was my turn to drive, after three laps, during which I lost so much time that we dropped from second to fifth place, I saw Harry out in the middle of the track frantically waving a flag to make me come into the pits so that he could drive again. We eventually finished second over-all and first in our class. I didn't learn to change gears properly until the chief mechanic of Maserati took me out and spent an afternoon teaching me."

Schell and Portago ran the 3-liter at Sebring in 1954. The rear axle went after 2 hours. He sold it and bought a 2-liter Maserati, the gear-shifting lesson thrown in, and ran it in the 1954 Le Mans, with Tomaso co-driving. They led the class until 5 A.M., when the engine blew up. He won the Grand Prix of Metz with the Maserati—"but there were no good drivers in it"—and ran with Chiron in the 12 Hours of Rheims, Chiron blowing up the engine with 20 minutes to go while leading the class. He ran an Osca in the G.P. of Germany, and rolled it. "God protects the good, so I wasn't hurt."

In 1954 Portago broke down while leading the first lap of the Pan American race in a 3-liter Ferrari, and won a class, an over-all, and a handicap race in Nassau. He bent an automobile occasionally, and he was often off the road, but he was never hurt until the 1955 Silverstone, when he missed a gear shift and came out of the resulting crash with a double-compound break in his left leg.

The crash had no effect on Portago's driving; he continued to run a little faster on the circuit and to leave it less frequently. At Caracas in 1955 he climbed up on Fangio until he was only 9 seconds behind him, finishing second. He was a member of the Ferrari team in 1956—an incredibly short time after he had begun to race He won the Grand Prix of Portugal in 1956, a wild go-around in which the lap record was broken seventeen times, the last time by Portago. He won the Tour of France, the Coupes du Salon, Paris, the Grand Prix of Rome, and was leading Moss and Fangio at Caracas when a broken gas line put him out of the race. After Caracas that year I asked Stirling Moss how he ranked Portago:

"He's certainly among the ten best in the world today," Moss said, "and as far as I'm concerned, he's the one to watch out for."

In Cuba, he was leading Fangio by a respectable margin when a gas line let go again.

"I don't think anyone will be champion as long as Fangio competes," Portago told me. "If the absolute limit of adhesion of the car through a certain bend is 101.5 mph, the old man will go through at 101, every time. I may go through at 99, or 102—in which case there'll be an incident.

"Moss is, of course, better than I am, too. If I pass Moss, I wonder what's the matter with his car! But I'm learning still, I think I get a little better with every race. I hope so, anyway."

Portago ranked Collins, Behra, Schell, Musso, and himself after Moss as equals. He carefully repeated his estimate of Schell: "Harry is very, *very* fast," and then said that he considered Schell his closest friend. They spent much time together. Both appeared to be tense—more accurately, taut—something that was not in any way allied to nervousness but was instead a peculiar expression of awareness. Like Portago, Schell walks rapidly; he turns his head constantly; he seems to be trying always to see something that is just out of sight, to hear something that is just out of earshot.

I said as much.

"It sounds corny," Portago said, "but I think that because racing drivers are very near to death every Sunday in the season, they are more sensitive to life, and appreciate it more. I take it that is what you meant by what you called "awareness" when you saw Harry and me walking together. Speaking now only for myself, I'm sure I love life more than the average man does. I want to get something out of every minute. I want no time wasted. You know, people say that racing drivers are dare devils who don't care whether they live or not, and you've seen stories about me and my flirting with death and all that. Nonsense, all nonsense. I want to live to be 105, and I mean to. I want to live to be a very old man. I'm *enchanted* with life. But no matter how long I live, I still won't have time for all the things I want to do, I won't hear all the music I want to hear, I won't be able to read all the books I want to read, I won't have all the women I want to have, I won't be able to do a twentieth of the things I want to do. And besides just the *doing,* I insist on getting something out of what I do. For example, I wouldn't race unless I was sure I could be champion of the world."

"Can you imagine yourself driving when you're Fangio's age?" I asked him.

Portago smiled. His mouth was unusually small and straight-lined; his smiles were brief, but warm enough. "Never," he said. "Certainly not. In any case I'll stop when I'm 35; and if I'm champion of the world, sooner."

"And then?"

"Well, I'm very ambitious," Portago said. "I wouldn't be racing automobiles if I didn't think I could get something out of it, and not only the championship . . ." The phone rang beside me. It was Portago's Caracas call, and I handed the instrument to him. I had passed the open switchboard in the lobby an hour before, when he had placed the call, and I had overheard the operator, so I knew to whom the call was going and that it would be personal.

"I'll take a walk," I told him. "Call me."

"Please," he said. "Don't go. Please. Anyway I'm going to speak Spanish."

As it turned out, the call was a report that the party in Caracas was unavailable.

"Forgive me," he said. "I didn't mean to be rude, I didn't mean to suggest that naturally you couldn't speak Spanish. I'm sorry."

I told him that he was right, in any case. "We were talking about what you intend to get out of automobile racing." I said. "I got the impression that you thought of it as preparation for something."

"I do," Portago said. "I haven't told this to a great many people. You see, Spain has had no new national hero for many, many years. That is what the championship of the world means to me. When I give up racing I'm going to Spain and go into politics."

Later, from Paris, Portago sent me a photograph of himself and Fangio and the Pretender to the Spanish throne. But on it he had written, "With Fangio and Don Juan, the *future King* of Spain."

The rumor that Franco intends to restore the Spanish monarchy has been current for several years. Portago seemed very sure. For all I know, he may have had superior information.

His frank statement of the purpose to which he intended to put the championship amused me. A few minutes before, he had been strongly critical of another driver who has some public business ventures: "He's commercialized himself so much," Portago said, rather disdainfully.

Still, one never expects consistency in anyone who gets his head above the ruck. Consistency is one of the marks of the drudge. Portago was, of course, a cynic, and I have no doubt he thought himself skilled in the management of other people —reporters included. If he did, it was a new idea for him, a product of the past 2 years, because he conceded that he had during most of his life been very shy, highly introverted, and that he had occasionally covered it with action that could be interpreted as rudeness. Certainly he was enormously perceptive, and conversation with him was easy and pleasant. He obviously knew that real conversation can concern itself only with *ideas*, not *things*, and I think that, like all first-rate minds, his natural preference was for ideas; he knew that it is necessary to listen, and he could be forthright, even in response to rough questions.

Portago was married in 1949 to the former Carol McDaniel, a South Carolina girl. They have two children, Andrea, six, and Antonio, three. Two hours after he had met Carol McDaniel, Portago told her he intended to marry her. He had discovered even early in life that women respond to daring as to nothing else—to daring, to indifference, to arrogance and certainty and sensitivity. In one sense, at least, women were more important in his life than anything else.

"The most important thing in our existence is a well-balanced sex life," he said to me. "Everybody knows this is true, but nobody will admit it—of himself, that is. But if you don't have a happy sex life, you don't have anything.

"It's the first thing the historians suppress when they write the lives of great men," I said, "and it was often an astonishingly big factor in their lives."

"Of course," Portago said. "Look at Nelson, look at Napoleon."

"Well, look at George Bernard Shaw," I said. "He gave it up altogether, and married on condition his wife would never mention sex to him."

"A freak," Portago said. "A very untypical writer. Look at Maupassant. A prodigy, in more ways than one. Well, as for me, making love is the most important thing I do every day, and I don't care who knows it."

Portago was willing to back up his opinions under most circumstances, whether by debate or a right cross. I had heard that he had once challenged a man to a duel, but he denied it. He fenced rarely, he said. He was taught boxing by Edmund Nelson, who died with him in the Mille Miglia. Nelson was a British ex-boxer who was just out of the Merchant Marine

Portago at Sebring in the 3.8—the car that "is against me." He drove ten hours out of the twelve.

and working in New York's Plaza Hotel when Portago, still in his teens, resided there. It was Nelson who taught Portago bobsledding—the first time Portago went down the St. Moritz run he went down steering, and he took 15 seconds off the time of the then-champion of Switzerland. It was Nelson who said, "I know Fon says he'll live forever, but I say he won't live to be thirty."

It is not on record that Portago lost many fights. He was always in condition. He ordered milk at most of the world's best bars. He smoked constantly, but never inhaled. His reactions were freakishly fast, beyond normal to an extent that even he apparently didn't appreciate. He once remarked after a car had spun with him, "It went very slowly. There was lots of time to think." Another time, speaking of steeplechasing, he said. "When your horse falls after a jump you look around for another horse to hide behind."

Recently in Paris Portago stepped off a curbstone as a Citroën went past, much too close, Portago felt, to the feet of the lady he was with. He flipped a cigarette at the driver so

quickly and so accurately that he hit him in the face with it.
The man got out and Portago knocked him down twice. He
handled his own defense in the consequent law proceedings,
and was thoroughly trounced by the plaintiff's attorney.

"I hate to fight," he told me. "I'll do anything honorable
to get out of a fight, but I get into situations in which there is
no way out. I was with some friends, shipping people, and a
man called them 'a bunch of bloody pirates.' I'm afraid I hit
him. Another time I suggested to a man on a dance floor that
it might be nicer for everybody if he put his cigar away when
he danced. He'd already burned a friend of mine with it.
When I started to leave the place, later, two of this cigar-lover's
friends stood in my way and wouldn't move. What could I do,
once I'd asked them please to let me by? I lowered the boom
on them."

We talked of a good many things that don't much matter
now, in the time that we sat in that room. It had rained hard
during the night, but the sun was steaming it off now. We
could hear cars slowing for the corner around the hotel that
led to the circuit. Two team Maseratis came past, the mechanics who drove them blipping their engines incessantly.

"Genuine Italian-type sports cars," I said, "suitable for
summer touring."

Portago grinned. "This is an easy course in one way,"
he said. "There's only one genuinely fast bend in it. But the
flat corners, the way it ruins brakes. . . . a race I don't like is
the Mille Miglia. No matter how much you practice you can't
possibly come to know 1,000 miles of Italian roads as well as
the Italians, and, as Fangio says, if you have a conscience you
can't drive really fast anyway. There are hundreds of corners
in the Mille Miglia where one little slip by a driver could kill
fifty people. You can't keep the spectators from crowding into
the road—you couldn't do it with an army. It's a race I hope
I never run in."

"I have a quotation in a story, a piece of fiction that

won't be published until this summer," I told Portago, "something that, I thought at the time, you might have said: Of all sports, only bull fighting and mountain climbing and motor racing really tried a man, that all the rest are mere recreations. Would you have said that?"

"I couldn't agree with you more," Portago said. "You're quite right. I've thought of bull fighting, of course, but the trouble is that you must start when you're a child, otherwise you'll never really know the bulls. And the only trouble with mountain climbing for me is the lack of an audience! Like most drivers, I'm something of an exhibitionist."

Portago and I had promised ourselves a certain length of time. We had run an hour past it when he stood up and I shut off the wire recorder. We shook hands and said good-bye. I saw him three times more, very briefly, before the '57 Sebring was over and everybody had dispersed. In April he sent me a note from Paris to say that he had won at Montlhéry, beating sports cars with a *gran turismo* car and breaking the lap record. He said he was going to run in the Mille Miglia and at Monte Carlo.

I did a draft of my story on him and sent a copy of it to him in Paris, as I had offered to do—but not before we talked. I'm not sure he ever saw it because I heard from him next from Modena. Finally, the day before the Mille Miglia, a cable came from Brescia, asking if I could use his first-person account of the race. Obviously he intended to live through the Mille Miglia now, although earlier he had written a note to Dorian Leigh, an internationally famous beauty with whom he had had a close relationship, that suggested a premonition of something happening: ". . . As you know, in the first place I did not want to do the Mille Miglia. Then Ferrari said I must do it, at least in a *gran turismo* car. Then I was told I had to do it in a new 3800-cc sports car. That means that my 'early death' may well come next Sunday . . ."

He told a reporter that he was intent only on finishing,

that it was important to him to come back to Brescia "safe and sound," an obvious reference to the fact that someone was waiting for him. But when he got out on the road, Nelson hunched enigmatically beside him, Portago began to go; he was fourth at the first check point. When a broken halfshaft put Collins out at Parma, Portago began to try for second place. He was straining for a sight of Von Trips' car, lying second to Taruffi, when the tire blew at something between 125 and 150 miles an hour on the straight at Guidizzollo. The 3.8 Ferrari, a model he loathed, lifted its wheels off the road and left him helpless. The car killed him; it very nearly destroyed his body; it killed Edmund Nelson too. When I heard he was dead, I looked for a note he had sent from Paris: ". . . I don't plan to return to the States until October. Please let me know where I can get in touch with you in New York, as we must get together at least for a couple of lunches . . . All the best, Fon."

Except for the final seconds after he lost the car, seconds that must have seemed so long to him, Portago's last hours were happy ones: Once he started running he would have set aside all premonitory fears; he was doing what he wanted to do, and doing it far better than the form-chart said he possibly could. He was surely thinking, as he screamed down the Valley of the Po toward Brescia and the finish, that he might conceivably win the race.

Most men die regretting the errors they have made in the multiple choices that life forces upon us, and Portago knew, in the fraction of time in which he could think about it, that error was killing him. Motor racing, like every other human endeavor, rigidly reserves the ultimate reward for those who are talented, lucky, and totally devoted. Portago was enormously talented, he was luckier than most, but he did not have, in the fullest measure, the vital ability to concentrate obsessively upon a single purpose. The gods, in whom he did not believe, or fortune, or fate or whatever, somehow guards those who *do* own this thing. Portago knew what it was, as

*Mille Miglia, 1957: Portago and Nelson ready to go off the ramp. This is
the car in which they died.*

many men do not. He often said that "you must have the mental strength to concentrate absolutely," but he could not maintain it as rigidly as, say, Phil Walters used to do, or Stirling
Moss does today. He did not want to run in the Mille Miglia.
A wiser man might have stayed out, even if it required an
illness of convenience. He had not made even one practice
circuit of the course, but he tried to outdrive men who could
not remember how many dozens of times they had run it.
Perhaps saddest of all, he overruled the Ferrari depot at Flor-
ence when he was urged to take two new tires for the run to
Brescia.

    In a sense, though, it is useless to think of what might
have been. Portago actually had no choice. There was no
caution in him. A refusal to count odds was the essense of his
nature. Usually, he won, but he was intelligent and he knew
that the averages would almost certainly trip him ultimately.

Knowing this, he still preferred to accept the hazard. That was his nature, the core of his being, and he could do nothing to alter it. Had he been cautious, we never would have heard of him. Portago's determination to take what he wanted out of the world—on his own terms and no matter what the price, present or potential—made him what he was: the absolutely free spirit.

"If I die tomorrow," he told me that day before Sebring, "still, I have had 28 wonderful years."

I cited to him the Spanish proverb, "In this life, take what you want—but pay for it."

"Of course," he said. "Of course, that's exactly it. You must pay. I remember someone who wrote about the British in the first World War, about the terrific mortality rate among young officers who had to lead bayonet charges against fixed machine guns. Most of them, or many of them, were aristocrats in those days. They had a life expectancy at the front of 30 days or something like that. And this man, he was a journalist, I can't remember his name, said, 'In war, the British aristocracy pays for the privileges they enjoy in peacetime.' You pay . . . you try to put it off, but you pay. I think, for my part at least, that the game is worth the candle."

Portago was not a great racing driver, although it is certain that he would have eventually become one, had he lived— and that is not alone my opinion, but the judgment of men much more expert. He was not an artist; he left nothing of beauty behind him, nothing of use to the world. He moved no mountains, wrote no books, bridged no rivers. He saved no lives, indeed, he took innocents with him to death. He could be cruel. If he wished to indulge himself, he would, even though the act might hurt and humiliate others who had done him no harm.

Yet, it would be a flinty heart that did not mourn his death. At the very least, he was an adornment in the world, an excitement, a pillar of fire in the night producing no useful heat or light, perhaps, but a glory to see nevertheless. At most, he was an inspiration—he proved again what cannot be reiterated too often. If anything at all is meant for us, we are meant to live life, there is no folly like the folly of the hermit who cowers in his cave, a dead lion is infinitely greater than a live mouse.

The accomplishments of the 28 years of Don Alfonso Cabeza de Vaca y Leighton may make only a small monument for him, or none at all, but he knew what greatness knows, and for that reason we are the poorer for his going.

9. The Indestructible Mr. D
by Dennis May

Never before the twenties, and certainly not since November, 1957, has there been a racing man like Fred W. Dixon; and beyond a shadow of a doubt the moguls of the Royal Automobile Club breathe easier for the fact. During a public life of nearly 35 years, the fabulous Freddie smashed more bones, broke up more saloons and ignored more laws than any other man in the British autoracing world. He also won as many races as, if not more than, any other driver of his era. But Fred was much more than a saloon-busting, car-crashing "leadfoot." Possessed of only the barest minimum of formal education, his services as a development engineer were in demand by virtually every important motor manufacturer in the United Kingdom. Fred was an engineer for engineers to follow, despite his near-illiteracy. He developed a host of innovations that are in use by racing men today. A pioneer in a field of pioneers, Fred could tune engines as well as an angel tunes a harp.

Perhaps one man in a thousand can be said to be a "survivor"; some one you can beat into jelly, whose bones you can break, who can absorb the punishment of days and nights of arduous labor—and still come back for more. You can batter him but you can't kill him. Such a man was Fred Dixon. In his first race he was tossed from his motorcycle while going over 90 miles an hour. He remounted and came in second. Another time his car catapulted 45 feet through the air; and on another occasion he was stopped cold from more than 110 mph by a stump. He lived and went on racing after each. Shortly after that he came through an airplane crash that would have smashed a lesser man; again, he went on to race. More than a decade after its last vicious swipe, the scythe that had swung so many times and missed reached out on November 4, 1957, and gently touched his heart. Even as most ordinary mortals, Fred W. Dixon died in his sleep.

If newspapers circulate in the hereafter, the meaty, scar-lined face of Fred W. Dixon must have creased into a grin as he scanned his obituary notices on the morning of November 5, 1957. For 46 years, divided about equally between the car and motorcycle fields, the deeds of this prankish genius had been supplying material for a veritable encyclopedia of legend and anecdote. And now, as the news went out that he had extended a noonday nap into eternity, automotive writers in Britain and the Commonwealth vied with each other in singing his praises and exaggerating his achievement.

The success statistics alone make an impressive list. Dixon was the only man ever to win all three Tourist Trophies—car, solo motorcycle, and motorcycle with sidecar. He was the

One of Dixon's few essays in supercharging, a blown 2-litre. Fred was the only man who could make the 2-litre Riley perform.

only driver to cop Britain's premier car classics of road and track, the T.T. and the Brooklands 500, in the same season. His over-all returns in the Royal Automobile Club's T.T. and the 500—two victories in each—were never surpassed while he held a license to race. His second 500 win, in 1936, was turned at a substantially higher speed than the same year's Indianapolis 500. In fact, his record had been topped only once before in the Hoosier classic, and then by .12 mph. His 2-liter Riley, reworked to the point where it was more Dixon than Riley, was by far the smallest displacement unblown car to score a 130-mph lap-speed badge at Brooklands. Fred was first to turn Brooklands at 100 miles per hour in a motorcycle sidecar outfit, years ahead of the competition. Although his claim was disallowed on a technicality, he was, *de facto,* at one time the fastest motorcycle rider in the world. Later, a machine he had built and mothered gained another "meteorcyclist" the official world speed title.

But it would have taken more than mere success to put Dixon on the high pedestal he occupied. They loved him for his defiance of every rule and convention in the book—social, legal, and technical; his generosity to the younger, less experienced, and financially poorer drivers who came to him for help and advice; his refusal to quit speedwork when, well on into middle age, his career was interrupted by a succession of really bad crashes; his unpredictable switches of mood, alternating between a molelike devotion to labor on the one hand and bouts of crazy hooliganism on the other.

Stuck with a tough technical problem, he would work almost without stopping for 4 or 5 days at a stretch, catching a catnap on the workshop floor every 20 or 30 hours, eating practically nothing and never noticing what he did eat, and even foregoing all alcoholic comforts in favor of mugs of sweet tea. Then, when the knot was finally unraveled, he'd break out on a marathon jag, drinking enough to pickle an octopus, calling on everyone within earshot to charge their chalices at his expense and wreaking havoc with the furnishings of all taverns on his erratic itinerary. The owners of these places seldom put up more than token resistance, first because they knew that Fred at play was about as amenable to reasoning and restraint as a rogue elephant, and second because he always came back afterwards and paid for the damage he'd done—sometimes for a good deal more than he'd done.

Liberal as he was with his prize money and other professional earnings, Fred was no fool. Even after paying for his expensive fun, he usually managed to return home a richer man from his continental capers. One of the few exceptions to this was an occasion when the promoters of a Belgian motorcycle race augmented their prize checks with gifts of FN automatic pistols. Before Fred was through practicing marksmanship, the doors, windows, and panelwork of his hotel and adjoining premises looked something like a collander.

It needed the sad event of November 4, 1957 to disprove the stock cliche that Dixon was indestructible. Certainly, in his lifetime he repeatedly lent weight to the fable, starting in 1921, the very first time he raced at Brooklands. This debut also sowed the seeds of his reputation for resource and improvisation. The race was a 500-miler for motorcycles—an experiment in endurance that was never repeated, owing to the inability of men and machines to endure it (only one rider per entry was permitted.)

Fred's bike was a big 61-cu.-in. Harley Davidson. By a mistake which was not revealed until afterwards, the steering geometry had been rigged for sidecar work, whereas this was a bachelor party. During training, then, young Dixon found it impossible to maintain contact between his butt and the saddle. So, taking advantage of friction, he scissored out a saddle-shaped sheet of sandpaper and glued it to the seat, abrasive side up. This dodge worked, but only for a while. Then, 90 miles or so after the start, he felt a painful sensation. The sandpaper had rubbed clean through his horsehide breeches and was eroding his backside at the rate of about a millimeter every two laps.

Thirty laps later, having in the meantime made a pit stop and dispensed with artificial aids to stability, Fred took a dive over the handlebars when the front tire left the rim at 90 mph. He rolled himself up into a ball in mid-air, then looped a dozen ground-level loops on hitting the concrete. He got up, miraculously, hobbled back to the Harley, kicked the bars and pegs straight, puttered to the pits on a bald front wheel, fitted a new tire, and resumed the *kampf!* He eventually placed second in a massacred field. Dixon, incidentally, was the only man to contest 500's on both two and four wheels. He was also unique in opposing the once-is-enough decision taken by the organizers of the 500-mile motorcycle grind.

A debut in a different school—his first car race—culminated in a crash so alive with drama that the eventual winner
hardly got even a mention in the headlines. The 1932 Tourist
Trophy, run over the old Ards circuit in Northern Ireland
was Britain's grandest *epreuve*. Fred was forty years of age at
the time and had quit motorcycle racing 4 years earlier. His
car was an almost-unrecognizable 1100-cc Riley that he had
bought secondhand less than 3 months before the T.T. and
completely reconstructed, with the sole exception of the engine-gearbox ensemble, in accordance with his own peculiar
ideas. That these ideas were effective was sensationally demonstrated when, in his first time out for practice, he not only
smashed the 1100-cc class record but also beat every 1½-
liter car in the list. As befitted the U.K.'s premier road race,
the field included official makers' entries from all the British
plants with an investment in speed, Riley and MG among
them.

It was against this background that a middle-aged roughneck from the barbarous north-country, with a car that visibly
proclaimed its bastard status, challenged the elite of British
automobile racing—experienced professionals, rich playboys,
titled seigneurs, the whole crowd.

It didn't take long to see who was going to eat whose dust.
Fred led during most of the first hour. Two hours, three hours,
and he still was out in front. Then, around the fourth hour, the
blackboard operator in his pit made a *lapsus calami*, hanging
out a signal that was a contradiction in numerals. Dixon, his
nerves at snapping point from lack of sleep (he had worked
throughout the previous night to cure a last-minute engine
fault) was heading into a sharp turn too fast to make it. Pointing the Riley at what looked to be the least lethal piece of landscape, he went off the road at 80, over-rode a shallow bank, tore
a tree out of the ground, and jumped a stream 10 feet above
water. In mid-air, as a sharpshooting photographer was able to
record, he had the presence of mind to switch off the ignition

as an antifire precaution, which evidently saved his life.

Landing 45 feet after take-off, the car incredibly stayed right-side-up; the driver's only injury was an enormous bruise on the broad backside that, 11 years earlier, had survived its ordeal by sandpaper. His riding mechanic, lacking Dixon's incredible streak of luck, cut his face open on the dashboard.

Another installment of the "Dixon is indestructible" fairytale was written in 1934 at Donington Park, England, scene of titanic Auto Union vs. Mercedes battles in the late 30s. Driving one of his full-race 2-liter Rileys, he was descending a fast slope to the circuit's one tight hair-pin curve when the back-axle casing disintegrated, carrying away both rear-break cables and snapping the propshaft. This time, all sections of trackside being equally dangerous, he slammed head-on into a tree stump, a foot and a half high and about the same in diameter, at 110. He returned to consciousness, with almost as many broken bones as whole ones and his already-battered face purpled with fresh scars, 10 days later.

That, he figured, would be enough for one season, and the surgeons nodded grave agreement. In fact, unless he could get his nerve back it might even be enough for one lifetime.

His choice of a nerve restorer typified the perverse streak in his nature. Hating airplanes ("The bloody things might fall down," he used to say) he took a plane up for the first time in his life. The flight achieved a momentum and altitude that was just sufficient to ensure total destruction for the machine and a severe roughing up for its occupants when it nosedived into the ground a moment after take-off. For the second time in months, Fred lay unconscious for 10 days.

One interesting point about the accident was that the fuel tank, mounted high up, had torn away from its moorings and crashed down on his head, spilling gasoline all over Dixon's insensible body. But the wreckage did not catch fire, amazingly enough. The odds were all in favor of flames breaking out, but they didn't.

As a conjurer of reliable, economical power from small, unsupercharged engines, Dixon was, in his day, positively without rival. His knowledge was entirely self-taught. His formal education ended in his thirteenth year. After that, I doubt whether, apart from technical works, he ever read what would be considered an intelligent book, and probably not a dozen books of any sort. His accent was gutteral north-country, only halfway intelligible to fastidious southerners, and he never sounded an *h* in his life. Yet, within a year of breaking into car racing he was getting come-hithers from automobile manufacturers who wanted him "on their team." As a born free lance he always refused these baits, recalling with wry amusement that prior to forming his attachment to Riley products, he had gone a-wooing around Britain's car industry, but in vain.

In a Dixon profile published in 1955 by *Motor Racing*, an English organ of speed sport, I tried to sort out the ingredients of Fred's genius. As nobody contradicted that analysis, and *M.R.'s* affable editors don't object, we will repeat it here. I think he owed his success to:—

Plain, straightforward engineering knowledge and experience.

An unusual capacity for sustained and concentrated thought, and a refusal to sidestep a problem until he had it licked.

An ability to see the job in terms of first principles.

A gift for orderly progression in applying his ideas, which he committed to paper before something else cropped up to crowd them out of his mind.

Disinclination to accept a practice or precedent merely because that was how it'd always been done in the best circles.

An unfailing turning to account of his failures and setbacks. Why did this or that happen? What was the lesson behind it?

Dixon in a rare moment of relaxation.

Many years before he turned to cars, Dixon was among the pioneers of one carburetor per cylinder on motorcycle engines; he applied the same system to every full-race Riley he built, fours and sixes both. In fact, it is probable that his larger Rileys were the first sixes to be rigged this way, certainly on the east side of the Atlantic. For all tuning purposes he regarded each cylinder as a separate engine, testing it individually on the brake and persevering until all outputs were precisely equal right along the firing line.

His carburetors were SUs by parentage but radically modified; the main difference consisted of using a single sliding-plate throttle (as featured currently on the D-Jag with fuel injection), giving an absolutely unobstructed gas passage and mathematically matched opening and closure. The carb bodies themselves were bolted permanently to a heavy, distortion-proof mounting plate; adjacent pairs shared a common float chamber. At a date when the behavior and condition of pre-carbureted air was a matter of apparent indifference to his rivals, Dixon had his SUs' intake mouths coupled to a sheet-rubber respiratory chamber of calculated shape and capacity, ensuring a cool, plentiful, and stable air supply.

As a result of these and other carburetion measures, together with hair-splitting exactitude in valve and spark timing, the Dixon Rileys not only outpowered all challengers of like displacement but set new standards of tractability and low gas consumption.

Fred was contemptuous of what used to be known as "sprint tune." So far as his Rileys were concerned, the phrase was meaningless: apart from axle ratios, he ran them in one and the same state of tune in all events on his schedule, meaning everything from the 500 down to a thousand-yard hill climb. Also, except when policy made it necessary to horns-woggle the handicappers at Brooklands, he invariably drove flat out from start to finish of any race or record bid, no matter what its duration. If an engine couldn't stand this treatment, he argued, it was time to find another that could.

Incidentally, in choosing to race the Riley six he acted against the advice of Victor Riley himself, head of the Riley plant. This mill had never been designed for speedwork in any case, and had in fact proved a flop in the few half-hearted attempts that Riley had made to whip a racing performance out of it. So far as the camshafts, pistons, manifolds, conrods, and carburetors were concerned, Dixon concurred in the makers' gloomy estimate of the design (for these components he designed and made replacements), but he nevertheless insisted that what was left had some merit. And how right he was!

Dixon pioneered the low-down, horizontal air-entry slot that is now a frontal feature of practically every racing car in the world. He came up with that one as far back as 1932, causing consternation among traditionalists who asserted that the proper place for a radiator was out in the climate, untrammeled with tinwork. It wasn't until 6 years later, when Daimler-Benz followed this lead on their Grand Prix cars, that the clicking tongues were stilled.

As well as drastically restricting the air flow to his radiators (notably on the four-cylinder racers), Fred broke away from another fallacious practice of the 30s by omitting all louvers and other breachings from the top and sides of the hood. This was done, first, to maintain an abnormally high air temperature around the cylinder head and upper part of the block (with beneficial results), and second, to direct the outgoing draft down around the crankcase walls, which louver exits would have enabled it to bypass.

That Dixon practiced what he preached about "sprint tune" was strikingly shown by the fact that at Brooklands he won his 130-mph lap-speed badge in the 500, of all races. Ultimately, he turned a lap on the 2-liter Riley at nearly 135, less than 10 mph slower than John Cobb's *libre* record on the 21-liter Napier Railton. The Railton and the Riley were the only cars to win two 500's each. In the 1935 marathon, before Fred's Riley cracked up during co-driver Walter Handley's spell at the wheel, Dixon himself had turned a faster lap than any recorded that day by Cobb's mighty bolide, which finally won at 121.28 miles per hour.

Fred's devices for ducking around irksome regulations were always good for laughs. To give himself enough thigh clearance in the pint-size cockpit of his 1100-cc track-race Riley, he sawed out the bottom arc of the steering wheel. It was then pointed out to him that the rules demanded steering wheels with a continuous periphery. It was that word *periphery* (they hadn't said *circumference*) that gave him an out. At the following meet he showed up with a wheel of the same shape as before but with the void bridged in with a straight bar. If the old one hadn't been safe, this one was just as risky, but it was technically unexceptionable.

His first car race of all, the 1932 T.T., brought out the "sea lawyer" in Fred. Because the T.T. was for sports cars, the carrying of a spare wheel was compulsory. Nonstandard bodies, on the other hand, were allowable, and the shell that Dixon planned was to be inches smaller than Riley's regular body in every dimension—so small, in fact, that there just wasn't room for a normal spare wheel in any undercover position; he didn't want to mount the wheel outboard because it would increase weight and spoil the good aerodynamic shape of the tail. His answer to this riddle was to buy an Austin Seven wheel at the junkyard and stow it with the tire deflated. It just went in. The rules, as he blandly reminded the furious strutineer, didn't say the spare had to be of a size and make that would *fit* the car, or that the tire must be pressurized. He had nothing to lose—a flat during the race would kill his chances anyway.

In the days when he was racing motorcycles Dixon had adopted a handle-bar windshield as a substitute for goggles. Like everything else he did, there was a good reason for it. Snaefel Mountain, highpoint of a bike T.T. circuit in the Isle of Man, was often capped in mist. In bad visibility he could take a succession of quick peeks out from behind his shield, whereas raising and lowering goggles involved taking a hand off the bars at perhaps 100 mph. After awhile, however, somebody pointed out that the regulations said goggles must be worn. So Dixon bought himself a pair and took the lenses out. Nobody noticed.

Of less than average height, he had broad shoulders and the muscles of a prize fighter. Around the tracks in his Riley

Dixon in the 1½-litre Riley, a car so finely tuned that it can be driven in a race and on the public roads with no changes.

days a favorite side show was his hoisting of a corner of the 2-liter car into the air and holding it there, 6 or 7 inches off the ground, while mechanics attended to some wheel or axle chore. During workouts in preparation for his 100-mph Brooklands lap record with a cycle and sidecar, the outboard wheel came off at around the century mark. Before the unsupported weight had time to hit the ground (it included a very frightened passenger who'd never ridden at race speeds before), he forced the machine over to an angle of lean where the sidecar was poised in precarious equilibrium 3 feet above the concrete. Holding it that way, he completed the lap without cutting the throttle.

By many and diverse methods, including substituting Elektron metal for many ferrous parts, Dixon trimmed the weight of his Riley sizes to levels that no track car of comparable lap speed had ever approached. This unique weight/speed ratio forced him onto a high-up strip of the bankings that had hitherto been considered the exclusive preserve of outsizers like Cobb's Napier Railton and Oliver Bertram's 8-liter Barnato Hassan. These encroachments repeatedly put him in wrong with the stewards, a panel with a predominantly elderly and stuffed-shirt membership. Fred's reaction to the ensuing reprimands and warnings was characteristic. If any steward thought he could get the thing around at 130-plus *without* using the high slopes, he was welcome to try.

Another time, after winning a race on one of the Brooklands road circuits, he incurred official wrath by ignoring the check flag and making several extra laps on an otherwise empty track. The stewards thought this was just another example of his incurable propensity for horsing around, and really let him have it. For once he gave them no back answers, maintaining what they probably considered an insolent silence. Years afterwards he told me the reason for this spree. The race was his first after being released from the hospital following his flying accident. The blow on the head from the plane's fuel tank had affected his eye muscles in a peculiar way. If he looked to right or left, it was only by a painful, slow-motion effort that he could focus straight ahead again. Oculists were consulted—and told him they couldn't do nothing to help him. Not being prepared to quit speedwork at the height of a lucrative career, he decided to drive an experimental race with his eyes trained along the centerline of the hood from start to finish. The effort was so successful that he simply didn't see the man with the flag, and remained unaware of his gyrations until the fellow almost threw himself into the Riley's path.

Luckily for the blood pressure of Brooklands officialdom, there was a Royal Automobile Club rule providing for the automatic withdrawal of a man's racing ticket if the law took his operator's license away. And this the law eventually did, for the rest of Dixon's days, following a highway contretemps in which he asserted his well-known individualism by socking a copper on the jaw. In addition to having the open road closed to him, he did a spell in jail, putting the stretch to a constructive use by livening up the carburetion of the prison cars. He also got permission to have draftsman's materials sent in and went to work designing one of the most remarkable automo-

Dixon (No. 16) on the high bank at Brooklands.

biles ever conceived to make an attempt at the land-speed record. He called it the *Dart,* which is exactly what it looked like
on paper. It was to weigh not much more than 3000 pounds and
had a planned speed of over 400 mph (this was about 12 years
before the late John Cobb set the 394.19 mph record that is
still unbeaten today). The 10-liter engine, which Dixon personally designed in detail, during and after his detention,
was of wobble-plate type and had the outward appearance of
a toothpaste tube; its cross-sectional diameter was somewhere
around 14 inches. The car was never built.

This was Fred's second abortive land-speed-record project.
Earlier, he had bought and experimented with the *Silver*

Bullet, a 1,200-horsepower jinx built originally for an L.S.R. bid by Kaye Don. Dixon finally decided that if the *Bullet's* transmission broke up, as it was apparently liable to, it would certainly castrate the driver and probably divide him geometrically down the middle. He therefore sold the car for scrap.

For sheer audacity as an engineering concept, the *Dart* was perhaps only equaled by the *Crab,* a vehicle that Fred designed and built during World War II and afterwards developed over a period of years. In the prototype form, in which I was once privileged to ride, it featured, *inter alia,* four-wheel drive, all independent suspension, a single brake on the transmission, and, most heterodox of all, center-point steering, like a kid's soapbox car. There were other variants that were even more radical: steering for both pairs of wheels and a device that automatically banked the wheels relative to the ground on turns. Even the prosaic sample I tried made conventional automobiles look silly, particularly in hill climbing—it would go up near-precipices without loss of traction—road holding, and braking. The upshot of this unique exercise was a long legal wrangle over patent rights that Fred either sold or didn't sell (don't ask which) to millionaire industrialist Harry Ferguson. A short while before his death, Dixon accepted an out-of-court settlement equal to about $40,000.

The last farewells to Fred Dixon were conducted in a way that would have warmed the life-loving old Yorkshireman's heart. A gang of his closer friends were invited back to his home to partake of traditional funeral refreshments following his cremation. After an hour they decided that it would be seemly to leave his widow to her grief, and prepared to take off.

"What!", she said, "leave while there's all this liquor left? Did you ever know *Fred* to do a thing like that?"

Come to think of it, they hadn't. So they didn't either.

10. Portrait of An American
by Steve McNamara

To some people, including many professionals, motor racing is as much a sport as a way of earning a living. Not so for a quiet, blond young man from California (now living in Florida) named James Rathmann. To Jim racing is strictly business and a very serious business at that; as a business it requires the same attention merited by any other commercial enterprise. The result, naturally enough, is that Jim Rathmann is probably the most consistently successful American racing driver of his time— when he chooses to run. Not for Jim are the barnstorming trips to the hinterlands to race on country fair dirt tracks, at least not any more. Jim is a specialist, a fast track specialist who drives only on such fantastically rapid venues as Monza, Daytona and Indianapolis. It wasn't always thus. Time was when Jim barnstormed the West and Middle West in a track roadster. Purses were easy then and promotors generous. To most of us roadster racing was as much a sport as a means of getting a dollar (which usually went back into the car), a sort of self sustaining hobby. Not for Jim Rathmann. Even as today, Jim was a professional. It showed. It showed in other ways too. It showed in an immaculate service rig—a small bronze painted pick-up truck and a similarly painted trailer for the race car. It showed in two fresh engines carried in the truck. Wherever and whenever there was a race, Jim was ready and he wasn't going to be hampered or delayed rebuilding worn or broken engines. The truck, trailer and roadster with its gold number 16 is long gone. Jim

Rathmann no longer tows his own car to the races. He doesn't own one. He doesn't have to.

Jim Rathmann is causing some mental anguish among those who believe they have American drivers pegged. Well-known on both sides of the Atlantic now for his convincing win at Monza, Rathmann's medium-size frame can't be squeezed into the standard stereotype of United States oval track drivers.

Who's to blame, Rathmann or the stereotype? Both.

The greasy, barely literate lead-foot who stands for United States DRIVER in the minds of many, bears approximately the same resemblance to the best American drivers as the obnoxious kid in the MG does to Stirling Moss. The best United States drivers keep their nails clean, speak the language like natives, write legibly and depend far more on judgment than guts. But given this revised version of the United States Championship car driver, Jim Rathmann still doesn't fit too well.

Quiet and unassuming to the point of secrecy, Rathmann is probably the last man you'd suspect of liking nothing better than driving 200 miles an hour. He spends considerable time in such bland pursuits as watching TV Westerns, fishing, and puttering around the yard of his ample home in Miami Springs, Florida. He isn't much of a party-giver nor goer and he shudders at the popular image of a race driver as a flamboyant daredevil who laughs at death.

"Bravery doesn't win races," he believes firmly. "It's good judgment and common sense. If a guy gets carried away and gets a little too much Dick Tracy in him, he'll wipe himself out."

Jim has great respect for his fellow drivers, both American and European. And he certainly doesn't belong to the school which insists the best oval track and road racing drivers have nothing in common. Rathmann subscribes to a view held by a couple of pretty fair country drivers, Juan Manuel Fangio

Rathman, tired, dirty, but happy after winning the Monza 500. A. J. Watson is on the right.

and Stirling Moss, that the critical faculty in racing is a highly developed sense of balance. Only if a driver can feel the car in the seat of his pants is he able to drive it skillfully. And the more sensitive his derrierre, the closer he can drive to the limit. Oval racing, a bore at best to road racing enthusiasts, does require the same sense of balance, the same ability to drive up to the limit.

Jim's attitude toward the automobile would seem a bit out of place at a regional rally: he sees it simply as a machine for driving as fast os possible, beating other drivers while doing it. This is of course the same motivation behind Grand Prix drivers. But in order to conduct this drive under the constant supervision of spectators, and consequently make money, American racing was promoted on small, oval tracks. It's the geography of the course rather than a lack of driving skill that has sapped United States racing of its interest for the sports car fan.

Rathmann fails to sympathize with the sports car enthusiast's disinterest in blinding speed as a method of earning a living, but he has a great deal of respect for the best Grand Prix drivers. During the feisty battle of words in the spring of 1958 concerning Fangio's ability to tame The Brickyard, Rathmann made his position very clear.

He said Fangio would be new to the Speedway, which is quite unlike anything else in the world, and would of course be at a disadvantage. "There are a lot of tricks to learn," Rathmann said, "but if he (Fangio) gets used to them he ought to do very well.

"And in one way Fangio will have an advantage. There's a lot of mental work in that race. You more or less have to keep talking to yourself or you'll go nuts. After driving in all those road races I don't expect Fangio would be the man he is if he didn't know how. He's been world champion five years. That means he's a great driver, period."

One of the drivers Rathmann liked and admired most was an Italian, Luigi Musso, and like all Americans who have been to Monza, he has great respect for the Jaguar drivers of Ecurie Ecosse.

While the terrific speeds at Monza in 1958 unnerved a few GP drivers (notably Harry Schell who had an ancient Ferrari), Rathmann thrived on it. Asked what he thought of driving between 200 and 210 on the "cobblestone" straights, Jim's principal observation was, "It's just fine, if you don't look at the trees."

Rathmann found in Musso a man with the same approach to racing. "He really put his foot in it going into those turns," Rathmann says. "He gave me a ride around the track in a Ferrari sports and I was terrified. He is—I mean was —a heck of a nice guy." And then Jim adds the ultimate accolade: "He was a real charger."

Underneath a polite, cheerful manner, Rathmann is recognized by his fellow drivers as perhaps the most fiercely competitive driver in America. This was evident during the last heat at Monza. Jim had won the first two heats and could afford to stroke the last, as Jimmy Bryan had done last year, finishing second or third, and still win the race. But any plan involving less than first had little appeal. Rathmann drove the last heat full bore, squelching Bryan's bid to win at least one heat.

There is an additional reason why Rathmann wanted to whip Bryan as soundly as possible. Although he is rated No. 2 to Bryan's No. 1 in the United States, Rathmann can well afford to believe he is the best driver in America. While Bryan drove nearly all of the championship races last year, Rathmann drove about half, yet going into the last race, at Phoenix, Rathmann held an ample point lead. But his car picked that point to poop out and Jim finished far back in the pack. Bryan won and picked up the No. 1 ranking.

The No. 2 on his racing helmet may bug Rathmann a bit, but the big spook in his life is the Indianapolis 500. Casual race fans know the 500 is a big race, but it's impossible to overestimate the almost mystic hold The Brickyard has on American drivers. In no other sport is there really a counterpart; no single contest that dwarfs all others. Even the United States driving championship is badly overshadowed.

Rathmann has driven in nine of the last 10 Indianapolis races and would be delighted to trade all those miles, and probably throw in a mortgage on his house, for a solid grip on the checkered flag. He's been close.

"In 1952," he says, "I had turned about 50 laps (of 200) when my brakes went out. Later I stopped for gas by grinding the car along the pit wall. An official saw what was going on and tried to shut off the car. My pit crew pushed him away and pushed me off. The best I could do was second." (With no brakes, yet.)

1953 was a close one of a different sort. Jim was boring down the front straight at about 170 when the crankshaft broke. "The car made three loops and went about 1,500 feet backwards. I ended up right in front of my own pit area. I said, 'Boys, I tried to get it as close as possible.' That was a hairy one."

His 1955 trip to Indiana was also memorable. "The car had an experimental two-way radio for talking to the pits. The day before the race I was running down the back straight at about 160 when I heard this voice tell me to go to some address and fix a stopped-up sink. They'd given me the same frequency as an Indianapolis plumber."

In 1957 "We figured we had it all wrapped up. But we put in too much gas toward the end and the car wouldn't handle. We were second by 20 seconds."

In 1958 Rathmann's car was clearly less powerful than most of the others, but he finished a respectable fifth by driving the corners much cleaner and faster than the other drivers.

So Jim Rathmann's a nice guy who doesn't knock the Europeans and is marvelously adept at driving in circles. What should make him of more than casual interest to the road racing follower? The possibility that he may prove or disprove a belief dear to the heart of the ovalphobe.

Rathman approaches the banking on the Monza high-speed oval. The car is the Watson-built Leader Card Offenhauser.

There is no more violent controversy than the transfer of skills between oval and road racing. The road racing fans insist Fangio in a good car would gobble up Indianapolis and Rathmann would be hopelessly outclassed at Monaco. The Championship car boosters take the opposite tack, with equal vehemence.

At Monza the road racers tried an oval track and some did quite well considering their machinery. But with a few exceptions, such as Musso, they didn't like it at all.

The opposite side of the coin, championship car drivers in Formula I machines, shows promise of reflecting more light on the controversy. Troy Ruttman signed to drive a Maserati (and did rather poorly in his first outing).

But Jim Rathmann is perhaps the most "delicate" of the championship car drivers—he uses his head more and his brakes less than most anybody else at Indianapolis. A fifth in the 1953 Mexican Road Race (behind four of 17 team Lincolns) indicates he isn't befuddled by long straights and abrupt turns.

Rathmann has the sense of balance (and balding pate) that seem prerequisite for road racing success. He can undoubtedly master the process of taking his foot off the floor long enough to shift gears. His performances at Sebring and Nassau were nothing to write home about—he drove hard but tended to treat the turns as if they were banked. However, Corvettes are hardly the machinery in which to establish a great road racing reputation.

Representatives of Ferrari and BRM thought enough of his talents at Monza to begin negotiations. (He was to drive a BRM at Rheims but the deal fell through at the last minute.) If the price is right Rathmann will probably join the Grand Prix circuit.

The attractions are obvious: Rathmann likes to drive fast cars and make money doing it. The United States sports car fan is aware of the generous purses and starting money offered in Europe and South America, but until fairly recently a surprisingly large number of American drivers believed the Grand Prix circuit was something akin to SCCA races with unpronounceable names.

Between turns around Monza's concrete soup bowl, the Americans discovered the Old World offers fast cars and money for driving them. Rathmann, who hasn't driven the complete American circuit in years, is very interested in the lucrative challenge.

It will be elucidating to see if the king of the Autodromo di Monza can make any headway with the princes of road racing.

11. A Comet Called Archie
by Donn Hale Munson

If ever a man was called upon to overcome handicaps to become a racing man, it was a young Scotsman named William Archie Scott-Brown. Few men have ever overcome handicaps as effectively and as gaily as he. Almost grotesquely short of stature, cursed with a withered arm and a limping leg, Archie stormed across and around the circuits of Europe with a slashing style that few men could equal and fewer still could surpass. Archie also had another quality that was equally amazing, all things being considered. A single vignette will suffice to illustrate:

The twelve hours of endurance at Sebring is, like any championship event, as much a show as it is a motor race and, like all good shows, it must have a "Queen," a pretty girl to decorate the side functions and, finally, bestow a congratulatory buss on the winner. But this time, March, 1958, something was wrong. The queen was missing. She'd been there all right, surrounded as usual by a cordon of officials and press agents, but now she wasn't.

They soon found her, having a ball. Scarcely 500 yards from the turmoil, she was calmly, happily sitting on a log with Archie. Punctuating their conversation were mouthfuls of bread torn from a loaf and washed down with swigs of Chianti.

The young lady can remain nameless. She only serves to prove a point: wherever you were, Archie Scott-Brown made you feel good. His gaiety had an electric quality about it. People automatically grinned when Archie walked into a room or a group—they couldn't help it, really, because the quality of Archie was infectious. His was a bright light, indeed, perhaps too bright. It shone for only a few short years and then, in 1958, it was snuffed out. The world is much the poorer for its loss.

The sleek, fierce Syracuse Connaught GP car howled down the straightaway, its driver sitting well forward but relaxed. The engine screamed defiantly as a final burst of throttle was fed to it. All over the Aintree pit area stop watches clicked as the car flashed across the start-finish line. Timers compared watches and startled glances.

"Two, three point eight . . . right?"

"Quite. Better than 2 full seconds faster than Tony Brooks. Don't know how that little bloke does it."

"Oh, Archie puts his foot in it. Very aggressive, y'know."

The Connaught wound down on a cool off lap and wheeled into the pits. The driver that crawled out looked anything but aggressive. Scant inches over 5 feet tall, he limped heavily away from the car, pulling off his helmet to expose long, wavy brown hair tumbled over a wide, smooth forehead. Behind his sunglasses gentle dark eyes crinkled in a fair-skinned face. A full-flowing "Royal Air Force" mustache curled upward at the corners of his mouth.

But these were the things you noticed only on close inspection—it was his rolling, limping gait, the width of his shoulders and the bulk of his biceps you saw first. Then you would notice that his right arm ended abruptly and tragically in a stub near the elbow.

Archie Scott-Brown looked like anything but one of the best GP and sports car drivers in the world. Yet, for almost 5 years he was to flash cometlike across the international racing scene to chalk up an amazing record, despite physical handicaps that would have chained a lesser man to a wheelchair.

He was born to an uphill fight in Paisley, Scotland, on May 13, 1927. The biological fates that bring genes together to produce the agile brain, keen intellect, superb reflexes, and sturdy bodies that go to make up great racing drivers played a dirty trick on William Archie Scott-Brown. They gave him the brains and spiritual make-up but put them in an incomplete body—one leg too short, one arm without a hand.

A psychologist would say that the force which moved young Archie was "compensatory." To make up for his handicaps, the little Scot faced life with fierce determination that showed even early in boyhood. He played a rugged game of rugby, charging hard and playing it smart to compensate for lack of speed.

To a psychologist it would be significant that, being retarded by his limp, he craved speed. A psychologist could also probably make something of the fact that one of the favorite games of the young Archie was "war."

He decked himself out in tin helmets, strapped wooden guns to his waist, and led imaginary troops into battle. A few years later he saw his friends go off to face the real thing during Britain's struggle for survival in the early days of World War II. He wanted, of course, to be a Spitfire pilot. But the RAF demanded physically perfect candidates. Archie stayed home.

The end of the war opened a way for the teen-aged Archie to find the speed he so fervently wanted. Gasoline rationing ended, and once again through England sports- and racing-car engines burst into their siren songs. Archie answered as best as he could, dicing the family sedan on back roads, competing in rallies, trials, gymkhanas, and any other event that would accept the entry of a boy who wedged the stump of one strong arm between the spokes of his steering wheel while he put his foot into it.

They began to talk about him in England, this young Archie Scott-Brown who could wheel an MG around a small-club circuit with the best of the postwar amateurs. On the course he would settle his thick-set, stubby body behind the wheel, gripping it strongly with his one hand and using his stump as a lever. He was lightning fast on shifts, slipping up and down gears with amazing coordination. What was most impressive was the way he kept the trottle well down. Archie wanted speed and he got it.

Search the records today and you will not find the name of the man who gave him his first real ride. But admiring English owners, reflecting their traditional respect for sporting ability—handicap or no—put Archie behind the wheel of fast cars. And he drove them to victory.

His first really big year was 1955. Here's the record:

First in sports cars at Snetterton, first in the British Empire Trophy Race at Oulton Park, first in 2-liter cars at Goodwood, first in unlimited cars at Snetterton and second in Formula I's . . . more victories at Brands Hatch, Crystal Palace, Charterhall . . . big cars, little cars, good car, dogs—Archie drove them all.

In 1956, Archie, sporting the big brown RAF-type mustache that was his personal trademark, went to Silverstone for the International Trophy Race. This is the first British Racing Driver's Club meeting of the year. The International is sixty laps—180 miles—around the 3-mile circuit.

The weather this May day is cool and dry. The course is fast and the big boys are here . . . Moss, Hawthorn, Salvadori, Schell, Collins, Parnell . . . yes! even the maestro himself, Juan Fangio. Is it possible the crippled kid has beaten down his handicaps to face company like this? He has!

Arch sits behind the wheel of a Connaught, a powerful and speedy Formula I job of $2\frac{1}{2}$ liters. Fourteen of the fastest cars in the world are on the grid. In the front row on the pole is Moss on a Vanwall. Beside him are Schell, also on a Vanwall, Fangio on a Ferrari, and Hawthorn on a B.R.M.

Collins (Ferrari), Salvadori (Maserati), and Archie make up the second row. Behind is the rest of the field . . . four more Connaughts, a Cooper-Bristol, two Gordinis, and a Maserati, all in the hands of ace drivers.

Archie and Peter Whitehead co-drove this Aston-Martin at Le Mans in 1958.

Electric starters moan dully and crews scurry to the track-side as engines catch and snarl. They rise in a screaming crescendo as the starter's flag rises and then suddenly drops.

Fangio gets off for a magnificent start. But almost immediately Hawthorn passes him. Archie puts his foot down but the front-row boys hold the lead spots. Hawthorn's B.R.M. grabs the lead for five laps, 7 seconds ahead of Fangio. Moss pushes the Argentinian hard and catches him. Round and round they go, power sliding through Copse Corner, twisting through Maggots Curve, Becketts Corner, and Chapel, and then, tearing down Hangar Straight to stand up on the brakes at Stowe Corner.

Archie roars into Club Corner, shifts fast, and tromps on the throttle again to barrel down the straight to gentle Abbey Corner, and then wrenches the Connaught through Woodcote Corner past the stands and pits.

The field shifts positions. Already, the old lap record has been shattered by almost everyone. This is the fastest race ever seen at Silverstone. The average speed is over 100 mph.

The pace is killing. Hawthorn's timing gear lets go and he is out. Now Moss leads. Fangio grimly follows him through turn after turn. Archie plays a waiting game because this is the speed that cripples cars. Sixty flashing miles later Fangio is out with clutch trouble and he screeches into the pits to take over teammate Collins's car. This mount lasts him only 12 miles.

Salvadori has slipped into second spot behind Moss. Now Archie moves, sticking the snout of the Connaught almost up on Salvadori's tailpipes . . . pushing, probing, forcing aggressively.

Moss's superior car keeps him out front. But Archie, boring in behind Salvadori's Maser, keeps the pressure on. And it soon tells! Salvadori roars into a turn, fights the wheel, loses it, wins control momentarily, and then loses it completely. The Maserati crashes.

Archie slips by, shaking his head sympathetically as he flashes a look at the wreckage. But now there's no time for sympathy. Moss is far out in front. Archie asks everything of the Connaught and she responds. But the lead is too great and 180 miles are over before he can close the gap. Moss wins at 100.47 mph. Archie is a close second.

The year continues with a succession of great races. At Goodwood Archie catches Hawthorn and leads. With Moss they make it a three-way race until Archie's car blows up in the final laps. That day he sees two friends die in action. Later, at Aintree, he turns in the fastest lap of the day, but an oil line snaps and he's side-lined. Bad luck begins to dog him.

It's the same story a few weeks later, again at Aintree. For eight laps Archie leads, but again oil blows back, forcing him out. Archie shrugs philosophically, "Ah, well . . . that's racing."

Racing—for Archie it is no longer a sport but has become a way of life, a chance to show the world that even if God has denied you one hand and made one leg shorter than the other you can accept the challenge and leave your mark in the company of the world's fastest men.

He won at Brands Hatch, setting a course record; the same day he jumped into an Elva with a special fiber-glass body to capture first place in a race ironically classified as a "handicap."

He won his class in the Daily Express Production Car Race at Silverstone, pushing a little D.K.W. at a terrifying average 70.76 mph. He won the 2-liter class on a Lister a few weeks later.

Meanwhile, he looked toward the Continent and bigger events. But European officials balked. No, his handicaps were too great. Let a man with only one complete arm race?

While English friends made appeals in high places, Archie went on racing. The dark helmet, dark polo short, and flaring mustache above gleaming teeth became a familiar sight on English courses. The spectators loved him.

"Blimey, what guts!" they said. And they were right. Guts at Silverstone, where his Lister-Maserati turned the fastest lap. Guts at Brands Hatch, Oulton Park . . . wherever the fastest company met to roar down the thin tightrope between triumph and tragedy, there Archie was to be found.

It was hot in the pits that March day in 1958 at Sebring, Florida. I leaned over the wall, watching my Corvette scorch off the line and dash away in front of the field. I could hear the thin snarl of the Lister Jags as the pack untangled from a Le Mans start on the 12-hour grind.

Archie was behind the wheel of one of the Jags. If I had a favorite running in that class, it was Archie. I was not alone. Archie clicked with Americans.

"A spot of brew, Archie?" we'd ask him in pre-race days at the end of tune-up sessions.

"Good show," he'd say and then accept an icy can and sit back to bench-race, the way drivers the world over do. Unlike many drivers, however, Archie was a very modest guy. I never heard him blame weather, his car, or other drivers for failures, never heard him claim personal victory when he won.

Now, between glances at the progress of the Corvette on which I was crewing, I watched Archie and his Jag.

It happened fast. Archie dove deep into a corner close to my pit and suddenly slowed. The engine had blown, and the car stopped, almost as if it had run into a patch of wet cement.

Olivier Gendebien, on a Ferrari, was close behind. He didn't have a chance. He braked desperately, but the Ferrari hurtled up the Jag's back and ground to a horrifying halt, one front tire sitting squarely against Archie's helmet!

Archie twisted in his seat, raised an arm, and flashed a big grin at Gendebien. The Belgian driver blinked, amazed. Archie waved him away. Gendebien threw the Ferrari into reverse, backed off the Jag, and tore away. Archie climbed out, unhurt.

"Oh," Archie calmly told me later, "odd sight, that . . . have a bloody Ferrari sitting on your head. I'll bet you guys all laughed."

"Oh, sure," I said, "it liked to kill me."

Archie stroked his mustache and squinted at the Florida sky. "On second thought," he said, "me, too!"

Months later, on a Spring night in a quiet bar 4,000 miles from England, two sports-car men were chatting.

"Read in the paper tonight that Archie got it at Spa, in the Belgian GP," one said.

"Flipped and burned. He was going like hell, really putting his foot in it. He really waited to make good on the Continent, you know."

"Yes. He was a terrific driver."

He was thirty-one years old when his comet burned out.

12. Singular Champion
by Denise McCluggage

On a rainy February morning in 1959 a green Jaguar sedan roared along a major English highway, rooster-tails of spray following it at the 90 miles an hour at which it traveled. Suddenly, sickeningly, it went into a long slide, skidded into an oncoming truck, and caromed off into a tree. It was demolished, and with it went the man who was perhaps the least likely candidate for a common road accident—the driving champion of the world.

Just before the accident that ended the all-too-short life and championship of John Michael Hawthorn, the following profile appeared in the pages of *Sports Cars Illustrated*. There is little that we can say here that its authoress, Denise McCluggage, has not said better. Mike Hawthorn was alive when the story was written. We'd prefer to remember him that way.

The late Marquis de Portago was passing judgment on various Grand Prix drivers and marking the ones he thought most likely to succeed to Fangio's throne. One famous name he dismissed with a shrug:

"He's too hard to classify. He's erratic. He seldom finishes. He never takes care of himself."

If Portago were alive, he would have seen the driver he voted least-likely-to-succeed become the 1958 driving champion of the world. But he would be not much more surprised than the tall, towheaded wearer of the crown, Mike Hawthorn himself.

Not that Hawthorn had not aspired to the championship. All drivers do. He had just never been particularly identified with the aspiration—not as his countryman, Stirling

Moss, for instance. Moss was called the "Crown Prince of Motor Racing," the obvious successor to Juan Manuel Fangio, to whom he was three times runner-up. With Fangio's semi-retirement, 1958 looked to be Stirling's year. But it did not work out that way. And thus to the son of a Farnham garage-owner went the honor of being the first World Champion from Great Britain.

"I'm glad to see old Mike pull this off," said a British enthusiast after the Grand Prix of Italy, when only a miracle in Morocco could salvage the championship for Moss. "He goes at this motor racing as it should be done. He doesn't give a damn." This, indeed, was the outward impression given by the big, square-jawed Briton. But whether under that indifferent surface lurked a will to win which would frighten even the most serious followers of the circuit is anybody's guess, because Mike Hawthorn was not a simple man.

Louise Collins said in Rheims a month before her husband's death: "Peter and I probably know Mike better than anybody else, and yet are constantly surprised by new moods and new faces. If you meet Mike in one mood, he will charm you—you'll absolutely love him. But if you meet him in another mood, you can hate him."

This moodiness, these many faces, were manifested in Hawthorn's driving. At one extreme he was capable of being almost mediocre and insensitively brutal to fine machinery. At the other extreme he was brilliant. There are those who say that at Mike's most inspired not even Fangio could touch him. And Fangio, that modest man, might well agree. The Champion from Argentina was quick to recognize the exceptional talent of the Englishman and said that, of all the drivers, Hawthorn was the one he most feared. Perhaps he was recalling the fabled 1953 Grand Prix of France at Rheims and the taut 3 hours of wheel-to-wheel combat, Hawthorn winning by inches.

Yet those who said, "Hawthorn is great—when he wants

All unknowing, Mike, soon to be World Champion, talks with Jack Brabham who, a year later, was to be Mike's successor to the world title.

to be," did not say it all. Hawthorn apparently had no con-
scious control over his "wanting to be." Hans Tanner, a
knowledgeable writer of the racing world, drove with Mike
during practice for the 1953 Mille Miglia. "There are two
levels to Mike's driving," Hans said. "On one level he is—
well, good. Very good. Always better than competent. But on
that other level, he transcends himself. He merges with the
car. He almost goes into a trance. And it has nothing to do with
what he consciously wants. On certain days, he simply has it
and that's all there is to it. And if you have ridden with him
on one of those 'second-level' days, you know you have ridden
with genius."

When Hawthorn didn't like a race, a circuit, a car—or
when he wasn't "on"—he would just as soon be out of the
competition altogether. Very often the car obligingly broke
down; not that Mike consciously set about sabotaging it, but
a car after all is a highly sensitive extension of the driver.
When the driver is not "on," he is at odds with his machine
as well as himself and a shift can be missed, a clutch slipped,
a car damaged, all too easily.

Mike did not at all like the Mille Miglia, for instance.
The first time he entered that classic, he had not gone far
before one of the master cylinders on his Ferrari gave out,
leaving him with only front brakes. He was far from unhappy
about retiring. (And then, on the way back to Modena, the
rear end broke.) No one could ever induce Mike to try the
Mille Miglia again.

He felt much the same about the Targa Florio, a race
around 48 miles of rough Sicilian roads, which he did for the
first time in 1958, and the 500 Miglia di Monza on the banked
oval. "Well, that's two things I've tried this year that I will
never do again," he said flatly after Monza.

After his first time out in practice at Monza in the 4.1
Monoposto Ferrari that had been specially whipped up for
the 500 Miles, Mike was trembling like an aspen leaf. "Did I

break the lap record?" he gasped (he hadn't been near it).

"Why are you trembling? Are you cold?" he was asked.

"Hell, no. I'm frightened." And he believed it. As it turned out, the trembling was muscle tremors from the unfamiliar effort of holding the Ferrari straight—its chassis was ill-suited to the bumpy oval. The trembling disappeared after he stopped fighting the car's every twitch and learned to permit the Ferrari to jump about like a spit on a hot stove. Still, he did not like Monza, and was delighted when "Uncle Phil," as he called teammate Phil Hill, took over the lion's share of the driving chores, with an assist from Luigi Musso.

Mike plainly preferred Grand Prix driving to any other kind. Long sports-car races do not bring out the best in him, although in 1955 he won both Sebring and Le Mans with a Jaguar. At Le Mans in 1958, when he shared a car with "mon ami mate," which is what he called his friend and teammate, Peter Collins, he damaged the clutch at the start—a common failing of his—and the car soon was well behind the leaders after a long pit stop. The weather was wet and miserable, too. "I cahn't se-ee-ee!" Mike complained after his first stint (he even stopped a lap too early), pulling his mouth down in that wide grimace that made him look like a fish going after a particularly well-baited hook.

Mike liked his comforts. Eschewing the limited facilities set up at the circuit, Mike dashed back to the hotel in town for a bath and a bit of rest when Peter took over the car for the second time. When he returned, fresh and little-boy looking, he exclaimed in mock horror to Louise Collins: "You mean to tell me Peter is still going around out there in this *rain!* The idiot!". At that moment, Peter returned to the pits, having deserted the now completely clutchless Ferrari on the circuit. "Well, mon ami mate, that's more like it." They shook hands and congratulated each other on relieving themselves of a wet and seemingly interminable task in time to get back to England by morning, and off they went.

Their apparent delight at having "broken" a car did not sit well with the powers of Maranello when it was reported back to the Ferrari factory. The "fair-haired" Englishers were not so fair of hair for a while. But the hand-shaking scene in the pits was misunderstood. It is ridiculous to think that the pair had conspired to damage the car and leave the race early. Both Hawthorn and Collins liked to win—liked to win very much. But neither were of the "press-on-regardless" school. Not like their teammate, Phil Hill, who in 1958 changed tires and literally moved a mountain (at the Targa Florio) just to finish. If winning—or at least doing very well—is out of the question, that mystic something in Mike that put him "on" used to snap "off."

But returning to Portago and his judgment on Mike, he was right—Mike was hard to classify, both in a car and out. Central Casting would never send him on a call for a racing driver. His flaxen hair and pink, choir-boy cheeks, would obviously be inappropriate. And then the technical adviser would throw him back as "too big" for a racing driver. Mike himself found his 6-foot-2-inch length a problem when it came to telescoping it into racing cars. His early cars were particularly small for him; he attributed his hunched-over, scrooched-down driving position to efforts to turtle into them out of the windstream.

There were many quickly identifiable characteristics that were "strictly Hawthorn": a bow tie and a blue helmet with a plastic rain visor (worn in the wet and dry) were two ever-present props. A car with a four-spoke steering wheel and minuscule amount of understeer probably belonged to Mike. Photograph a driver in action whose mouth is constantly drawn and distorted as if in torture (the fish-after-bait look) and you would have a picture of Mike.

Off the course, a heavy-tweed, slant-pocketed sports coat, a chewing-gum-colored corduroy cap bent until peaked like a rooftop, and again a bow tie, all set upon a figure talking to a

Pensive, Hawthorn in his "trademark" corduroy cap with crushed peak.

crowd of ever-present, ever-admiring—and admirable—females —this would have been Mike. Sprawl an apparently disinterested driver behind the pits reading the ubiquitous Western paperback while out front mechanics and team manager flew into dithers over his ailing machine, and that was sometimes Mike. Fill a room with a laugh that started from the floor, free and loud, then broke a wide face even wider making others turn from their conversations to smile, and that was Mike. Watch a man with a strong face grown grave and distant, holding in his hands the crushed helmet of a friend about to die, and that, too, was Mike.

Mike was a unique and interesting person, as changeable as the fortunes of a race, and sometimes a little zany. After Sebring in 1958—his car had retired—he had a head start on celebrating the victory of "Uncle Phil" and "mon ami mate."

Mike decided to take a bath in the Collins's motel. This was perfectly all right except that he chose to do it fully dressed, shoes and all. They found him in the tub as he gaily lathered his clothes.

Mike was sometimes a captive of his own sense of humor. At the 1000 Kilometers at the Nürburgring last season, Mike jumped the gun on the Le Mans start and was halfway across the road before the countdown was finished. From behind him came the irate scream of his friend, long-recognized King of the Le Mans Start, Stirling Moss: "You b.................... Hawthorn!!" It was too much for Mike; he doubled up with laughter right in the middle of the track. Moss and the rest of the pack dashed past him. In tears from laughing, he was almost too weak to start his car once he reached it.

There were many "firsts" in the life of John Michael Hawthorn starting the tenth day in April, 1929, when he first saw light of day. His father, Leslie, was a garage owner and a man active in motorcycling and motor-racing circles, so Mike was close to this world from the time he was a tyke.

His first time at the wheel of a car was at the age of eight, when he "borrowed" an old Jowett that had been left for repair. With the car in gear and its engine off, he ground it around a field behind the garage on the starter motor.

His first vehicle was a 1927 Norton motor bike, which he owned when he was 14. Since he was too young to drive on the road, this vehicle was for tinkering only.

His first brand-new machine was a 1947 350-cc. Competition B.S.A., and it was with this that he made his entry into motor racing. In his first event he won an award, the Novice Cup.

His first competition car was an 1100-c.c. ex-factory Riley Ulster Imp. His first entry into competition with it was at the 1950 Brighton Speed Trials in which he won his class.

His first season in a single-seater was 1952, when a friend of his father's bought a 2-liter Cooper-Bristol for him to run.

His first entry into a Grand Prix was the same year. It was the G.P. of Belgium at Spa, and he was fourth in the

Cooper-Bristol. His first crash was at Modena in his Cooper, when he went there to drive a Ferrari (his first trial for that *Scuderia*). He was not seriously injured and neither was the impression he had made on the Ferrari executives. At the end of 1952 he became the first English driver since Dick Seaman to sign with a continental racing team.

When Ferrari signed him, Mike was just twenty-three years old. This was a mere 2 years beyond his first "go" at Brighton, but 6 years before his championship at Morocco. There was to be a fabulous first season just ahead of him, but it was to be followed by 4 up-and-down years during which he was dogged by several crashes and severe burns; a kidney operation; the death of his father, to whom he was extremely close, in a road accident; the death of a very close friend in another accident; the grim tragedy at Le Mans in which he was the first link in a chain reaction; and the frustrations of driving G.P. cars (Vanwall and B.R.M.) which were still in the early stages of development and, although capable of leading, seldom able to finish.

Mike's first year with Ferrari, 1953, was probably one of the most successful rookie years ever. In his first three races for the prancing horse he finished fourth, third, and second. Then came the Grand Prix of France, which was the high point of the season and perhaps of Mike's entire career. Certainly it was one of the most exciting Grands Prix ever—in Rheims they still suck in their breath when it is mentioned.

At the midway mark of the race, there were still seven cars running under a blanket. And look at the fast company this young Englishman was keeping: The order ran Fangio, Hawthorn, Ascari, Farina, Villoresi, Bonnetto, Gonzales. Gonzales had been leading until he stopped for fuel. Then the lead proceeded to be passed back and forth between Hawthorn and Fangio. A report at the time said the lead changed no less than twelve times.

Every spectator was on his feet, tense, and the pits were

in an unbusinesslike frenzy of excitement. "We would go screaming down the straight, side by side absolutely flat out, grinning at each other, with me crouching down in the cockpit, trying to save every ounce of wind resistance," Hawthorn says in his book, *Challenge Me the Race*. "We were only inches apart. I could clearly see the rev counter in Fangio's cockpit."

Dicing with Fangio is one thing; crossing the finish line ahead of him is quite another. Mike knew that if he left the hairpin turn onto the pit straight just ahead of Fangio, Fangio would slipstream him and then nip past just under the flag. He knew, too, that Fangio was too wary an operator to let a "new boy" slipstream *him*. Hawthorn found the impetus he needed out of the final turn by slipping down into first gear and literally blasting his way out of the turn. He raced Fangio across the line by a second. And Gonzales finished only a few feet behind Fangio and Ascari some 3 seconds behind him. *The Autocar* reported: "It was a battle which exhausted even the spectators with its intensity and duration."

Hawthorn's second year with Ferrari was much different. Early in the season he was painfully burned in a crash with Gonzales at Syracuse. Then the news of his father's accident reached him at Le Mans. And when he returned home to England for the funeral he found himself the center of a to-do over whether or not he had been dodging his military service. (He had at one time been deferred as an engineering student.)

Press, public, and even Parliament took up the matter. Mike was never one to explain himself or go out of his way to smooth ruffled public relations. He remained true to form, and the storm raged. As it turned out, he would have been deferred on physical grounds, if not because of his burns then because of his kidney condition. He was to go into the hospital for surgery for that soon, but not before he went to Barcelona and won the Grand Prix. That, and the Supercortemaggiore, a sports-car race, were his only victories for the year.

In 1955 Mike and Ferrari parted company, not too amicably because no one parts amicably with Ferrari. The *Commendatore* is a strong man. The disagreement was over Mike's wanting to race for a home team, Jaguar, in the limited program they had scheduled and drive Ferrari in the Formula I races. Ferrari did not wish to share him, so Mike chose Jaguar.

He won Sebring with Phil Walters in Briggs Cunningham's D-Jaguar, but it was not an unclouded victory. The laurel wreaths and congraulations first went to Phil Hill and Carroll Shelby, who shared a Ferrari; then a re-check of lap charts gave Jaguar the victory.

But the Le Mans victory with Ivor Bueb was even less joyful. That was the year Pierre Levegh's Mercedes Benz hit the wall across from the pits and sluiced through the crowd, cutting a swath of fire and death. The Mercedes had dodged an Austin Healey, and the Austin Healey had spun in dodging Hawthorn's Jaguar as Mike cut sharply to stop at the pits which lined the all-too-narrow roadway. There was no room for dodging.

Eighty people died in this disaster. Hawthorn was quickly cleared of any responsibility for the crash in the investigations that followed, but the press—particularly the German press—did not let the matter drop. Perhaps in an effort to disprove opinion that the Mercedes' magnesium body burned with abnormal intensity and to disprove the wild rumor that the car had carried a secret, highly volatile fuel, the German papers overemphasized Hawthorn's part in the chain of events that ended in the Le Mans tragedy. Because of Le Mans, Hawthorn was, at best, a controversial figure in Germany until his death.

Hawthorn's popularity in Germany was not enhanced by his being black-flagged for passing "dangerously" and bumping a Porsche in the tail during the 1000-kilometer race at the Nürburgring in 1956. The same year, Hawthorn was refused an entry in the G.P. of Germany. The insurance companies refused to cover him, it was said. This caused a great ruckus in the motoring world, and many letters to editors in many languages. But since then, as Richard von Frankenberg, the noted German journalist and driver has said, "the waves have calmed."

On top of everything else, 1955 was Hawthorn's darkest as far as Grand Prix racing was concerned. He failed to collect even one point toward the championship. He was driving for Tony Vandervell at a time when the Vanwalls were not completely through their growing pains. Vanwall, like Mike, still had 3 full years to go to its world championship.

The next season, 1956, Hawthorn did not do much better, earning only four points. It was another year of experimentation and development for Vanwall—and for B.R.M. Hawthorn had three incidents with the latter, all of which could have been very serious. During a test, once, the hood flew off and dealt Mike a terrific blow on the head. Had it struck at a slightly different angle, he would have been decapitated.

He also rolled a Lotus this unhappy year. He partly made up for the frustrations on the circuits by taking to the air and earning a pilot's license. He flew to many of the races in his own plane.

Back home again with Ferrari in 1957, Mike fared much better—finishing fourth in the championship—but by no means coming near his 1953 season. Ferrari was in transition from the last legs of the Lancia-Ferraris to the fantastic new Dino Ferrari, which was still many months from completion. The old cars just weren't up to the best of Maserati and Vanwall. At the Grand Prix of Rheims for instance, the Ferraris could not even equal their times of a year before. "That's what I call progress," Peter Collins grumbled. "A year of improvement and we're 2 seconds slower." He grabbed a paperback Western and retired to his station wagon. Mike agreed, unfolding out of his car: "As far as I'm concerned, they can burn them," and he grabbed another Western and joined Peter.

The high point of that year was a defeat at the Nürburgring. Collins and Hawthorn were well in the lead, playing at

Hawthorn in Ferrari leading Steward Lewis-Evans in Vauxhall on the South Curve at Monza in 1958.

racing, after Fangio had stopped his Maserati at the pits. Then, suddenly, they received signals from the pit that the Old Man was back in the race—and he wasn't dawdling. They pushed as hard as they could, but Fangio kept cutting great chunks from their lead, and from the record, too. Driving the race of his career, Fangio charged on, caught the two Ferraris, and beat Hawthorn across the line by 3 seconds, thus evening the score of a game begun several years earlier at Rheims.

In Mike's championship year of 1958, Portago's charge of "erratic" could scarcely hold. In fact, Mike had been, if anything, dully consistent. He scored points in all the Grande Epreuves he entered except one (the G.P. of Germany). He finished all but two (Germany and Monaco). He had fastest lap four times. He won only one race (France), and he was second a total of five times. And it was not an easy year to be consistent. Mike witnessed the fatal accidents of two teammates—Luigi Musso and his "mon ami mate," Peter Collins.

Compare Mike's record with Stirling's. Moss finished only five races, but he won four of them and was second once. He, too, had fastest lap four times. With the best six races counting, Mike put together a score of 42. Stirling mustered 41.

Apart from the fact that Stirling just did not finish enough races—sometimes it was his fault and sometimes it was the car's—the fastest laps told the story. If any one "fast lap" in particular told the story, it has to be the one at Portugal.

Moss won Portugal. Hawthorn was second and had the fastest lap. During the race, Moss thought that he had the fastest lap because of a misunderstanding of his signals from the pits. There was a sign shown to him that said: "Haw. Rec." It meant Hawthorn just made a record lap. Moss read it: "Haw. Reg." which meant Mike was "regular"—not gaining time, not losing it. If Stirling had not misunderstood the sign, and if he had made fastest lap and if—. But as they say over there, "with if, you can put Paris in a bottle."

And that sign, "Haw. Reg." that Stirling thought he saw. That was the answer to the entire season. Hawthorn *was* regular.

Editor's Note: Mike Hawthorn had little chance to enjoy his championship or its fruits. As 1958 became 1959 Mike died in one of the most ironic tragedies ever seen in the racing world. Hurrying to London on business in his tremendously fast Jaguar sedan, Hawthorn went into a long slide on the rain-slick pavement, brushed an on-coming truck, and smashed into a tree. An accident on an ordinary road thus took the life of the 1958 driving Champion of the World.

13. Racing's Unloved Genius
by Simon Bourgin

To those familiar with international racing there is one
figure that is recognizable in any picture from any angle.
That figure is the one belonging to the most fabled and
successful *rennleiter,* or racing manager, of all time.
Grumpy, rumpled, infinitely painstaking and virtually
impossible to please with anything short of an absolute
win, Alfred Neubauer has led more racing teams to victory
over a longer period of time than any other man. The
anecdotes and tales that have gathered themselves around
"the fat man of Untertürkheim" would fill a book and
only a small percentage of them would be apocryphal.
Alfred Neubauer left nothing, absolutely nothing, not
even the smallest detail, to chance as he drove the men
of the mighty Mercedes racing teams to victory-winning
performance. Everything was planned in advance with
an efficiency that was virtually machinelike. It was he who
oversaw the practice sessions and it was he who led the
drivers of Mercedes in post-practice and pre-race skull
sessions. Alfred Neubauer knew every track as he knew
the top of his desk. He knew more about his opponents'
cars and equipment than they knew themselves. He knew
their weak points and their strong points, foreseeing every
eventuality and holding an answer ready for every one.
His memory is absolutely prodigious. Take any given
track and Neubauer can tell the finishing times and lap
averages of virtually every race ever run on that venue.
Few people know that Alfred Neubauer was once a driver
himself—a good enough driver to have been brought to
Mercedes in that capacity. It is perhaps due to that very

efficiency that is the soul and being of the man that he
was a driver only for a short while. When he could train
himself to no finer edge he stopped. It was more efficient
to train others, to push more skillful hands and feet than
his, to combine his efficiency with that skill to produce the
greatest racing teams the world has ever seen.

Alfred Neubauer, has a right to consider himself a frustrated man. For 26 years he led the greatest racing team in
automobile history. His knowledge of cars and drivers was
considered unparalleled and was a jealously guarded Mercedes
asset.

Yet today, Neubauer, in charge of the private drivers'
section at Mercedes, is sharing his precious knowhow with
anybody who wants it. Now that Mercedes has quit the racing
field, Neubauer's new job is to help amateur drivers prepare
for races. Any Mercedes driver who takes the trouble to find
Neubauer at the Stuttgart factory can now consult what is
probably the most experienced mind in automobile racing,
and on the company's time.

A few of these who have are Kurt Reiss, owner of a German canned goods factory, and Rainer Guenzler, a German
radio reporter. Anxious to enter racing, these amateurs have
gone to Neubauer for advice on improving their cars.

This is a far cry from presiding over Juan Manuel Fangio,
champion of the world, Stirling Moss, champion of England,
and Karl Kling, the best driver in Germany. This prize-
winning combination, with Neubauer as chief, constituted a
"dream" team. Broken up when Mercedes left racing, it was
probably the finest team ever assembled.

But far from being frustrated, Neubauer at his new job
is a happy man—or as happy as this scowling, cantankerous
figure permits himself to be. In addition to advising amateurs,
he is still training drivers. an essential of life for Neubauer.

Grand Prix of France in Reims: Rennleiter Alfred Neubauer orients his drivers. Woe unto the driver who doesn't pay attention!

Perhaps Neubauer is tranquil at his new job because of the enviable record he established in the last one. Returning to racing in 1952, the Mercedes racers under Neubauer scored an unprecedented number of wins. In 1954 they scooped the British Grand Prix race for the first such quadruple victory in history. "Today's race," reported a correspondent there, "was simply another demonstration of the superority of German racing cars. Mercedes entered four and the four, with never a pit stop, finished first, second, third and fourth."

In fact, Mercedes by the time it left the racing field had become to the sport what Rocky Marciano was to boxing—a combination of stamina and preparedness that could hardly be beaten. Much of the credit for this belonged to Alfred Neubauer. His method was to test actual performance in advance. No expense was too great: a sample test session might include six drivers, 20 mechanics, one secretary, two engineers and a dozen assorted technicians. These were assembled for a single purpose; to produce the performance reports that are a racing chief's life blood. Shock absorber settings, oil pressure readings, tire wear and gas consumption are dull things, but taken together they make possible the improvement that later wins races.

A master among appraisers of such facts, Neubauer on the job looks and acts anything but the conventional expert. He was once observed beginning the day at the Nurburg Ring track in Germany and was described thus: "In his left hand he clutched a briefcase bulging with data. His right hand held a partially empty bottle of "Pott Privat 54," a harsh German whiskey that he had taken the first nips from at breakfast. Facing his drivers and mechanics, Neubauer barked: "3,800 kilometers, that's what every driver has to do, and I don't give a damn if he likes it or not."

Fat men are usually jolly, and Alfred Neubauer is a fat man. He weighs 265 pounds, and has a 58-inch waistline. His waistline, in fact, is almost as famous as his capacity for drink. Neubauer's customary liquid intake with dinner is two gins, four beers, and two bottles of wine. Between dinners he works away at a bottle of "Pott Privat 54." Drink does not, however, slow him down. Nor does he give the impression of being anything but collected at all times.

Unlike other fat men, Neubauer is not a joker or a funny man. His closest approach to humor is to tease. He asked Stirling Moss for months why, since his pet Maserati racer was always breaking down, he didn't send his pay directly to the Maserati factory.

The view that Neubauer takes of life is dour, and he is regarded dourly by many of his colleagues. He is liked by some, but it would be hard to find anybody in racing who loved Alfred Neubauer. Neubauer's rudeness is proverbial; sometimes he is merely brusque, as when he awoke a driver two hours early with, "Man isn't here to sleep, but to live." His contemptuous remark to a mechanic about to garage a car —"Can you drive?"—is more characteristic.

He regarded his drivers as nobles who should not consort with ordinary mortals. The Neubauer table, whenever the Mercedes team was dining, was a closed circle—woe to outsiders who pulled up a chair without invitation. In fact Neubauer brooded over his drivers like a clucking mother hen. He ordered their food and drink, and told them when to arise.

Neubauer's conversation, conducted simultaneously in German, French and English, the languages of his drivers, pours forth like a torrent. It is 90 per cent concerned with cars, 10 per cent with women. Those who listen collect such nuggets as these. The object of racing: "To get the sport of driving from the race tracks to the highways, that's what we're after." Mass production of cars: "I'm against it. To make a car as individual as possible, to give it its own character—that's sport."

He dislikes being interviewed. Said Neubauer to a journalist who wanted to write his life story, "Don't ask me any questions if it concerns cars. As for your book, I'm writing three myself—and don't ask me about what."

This attitude has not endeared Neubauer to the press, and some of his own company officials speak of him as "difficult." But it is not Neubauer's aim in life to be liked. He is single-mindedly and passionately devoted to improving the performance of Mercedes automobiles. This preoccupies him totally.

He has certainly been successful. In racing Neubauer is regarded much as the late Knute Rockne used to be in football—a giant in his field.

Chief among the qualities that have won him this regard is a vast Teutonic thoroughness. Under the Neubauer regime, every detail is planned in advance—nothing is left to chance.

Added to this is a colossal memory. "Neubauer can tell you," said a driver, "about every race a Mercedes has ever been entered in: the driver, the time, the condition of the car, the other drivers and their cars, plus the barometric pressure and the temperature of the road and air that day. Altogether not a bad man to have around."

But it was in the race itself that his enormous experience was put to acute use. "He was the key man," said Stirling Moss of him, defining the racing chief's role. "He fixed the strategy of the race. It was Neubauer who set the pace and who by signals to the drivers and mechanics decided if the race should go faster or slower.

The pace that Neubauer set was best described by someone who watched Moss and Fangio leading the field in the British Grand Prix and Aintree. "Both sat in their cars with the comfortable ease of chauffeurs at a wedding, and yet the pace they set was so fast that the opposition fell to pieces around them."

As the race proceeded Neubauer watched from the pits. The fourth silver Mercedes was trailing a red Maserati for fifth place. As the Mercedes driver, Pierro Taruffi, sped by, Neubauer signaled him: beat the Maserati. Taruffi hounded the Maserati till, blackened with its exhaust, he inched by to take the lead. He came in fourth to give Mercedes a clean sweep and to establish, in Neubauer's sight, the right order for the day.

Neubauer feels that no racing chief can know his job unless he has been a driver first. "Otherwise you can never know what the driver is up against." But while Neubauer was a driver—in 1924 he was third in the Targa Florio, 13th in the Coppa Floria, and second at Semmering, a fierce test of uphill climbing—he was not a very good one. "He thought he was fast at Semmering," says somebody who was present, "but his mother scolded him for not doing better."

The remarkable fact is that he still drives for speed,

Neubauer was once a driver in his own right. He's seen here before the Targa Florio in 1924.

even occasionally. The size of his paunch prevents Neubauer from tying his shoelaces. Yet just two years ago he drove a Mercedes 300 SL around the Nurburg Ring. "He had to get in with a shoe horn," remarked another driver admiringly, "but he drove it fast."

Mercedes pre-eminence in racing did not come cheaply. It used to cost the company four million dollars a year to be represented on the race tracks: the approximate cost of maintaining the famous Racing Division with its 260 employees. Now that Mercedes is out of racing, no other company spends anything like it. Why, with the superiority of their cars proven many times, did Mercedes do so?

Neubauer's answer is to the point. "It sells cars. The public has to be educated in cars that are individually produced. We can't advertise in newspapers all over the world, but we could enter races all over the world."

Today, says Neubauer, the formula has changed. "Now one reaches peaks of performance to transfer *parts* of experience into practice. How far can you carry this thing? Well, it's like working for your doctorate—it shows you are trying to improve."

The chief point, Neubauer adds, is that racers don't stand still in development. "Our 300 SL reached 260 kilometers per hour on the Frankfurt autobahn, so we can say it was tested for that. The Volkswagen, which goes 66 miles per hour, doesn't need testing—it stands still.

"Sure racing costs money. But we gained advertising and experience.

"General Motors and Ford might sell more cars too if they raced. But they don't need to. Under the United States system of mass production, the product speaks for itself. We have to prove our product is good."

Fortunately for the public, says Neubauer, a company doesn't like to see its car break down in a race. The result is enormous planning and a close check of performance.

"So the public benefits. Look at what today's racers have that are bound to be absorbed on tomorrow's cars. We have fuel injection, speeds up to 10,000 rpm, the new single-joint rear axle—which we've transferred to our '220' and '300' production series, and tires that wear only two millimeters per 500 kilometers as compared with prewar tires that were finished after only 120 kilometers."

Of course, says Neubauer, the evolution of the car has differed in the United States and Europe. In the United States the sports car gets produced out of sheer public demand—racing has nothing to do with it. "But here in Europe it's the other way around. This year's racer becomes next year's sports car. And the improvements on the sports car later get transferred to the touring car."

It was a Mercedes driver, Pierre Levegh, whose racer, wrecking freakishly at Le Mans, caused the loss of 87 lives. Understandably the Mercedes staff have strong feelings about an issue which has rocked racing since that time. Are racing speeds today suicidal? So great are the risks for drivers and public, it has been claimed, that racing is no longer sport.

The Le Mans disaster cost Mercedes the race. Though

In one of his rarer moods, Neubauer happily hugs Sterling Moss (right) and co-pilot Denis Jenkinson after their Mille Miglia victory in 1955.

holding a seemingly incontestable lead, the Mercedes racers were withdrawn upon instructions from Stuttgart, out of deference to the terrible toll of lives. "The race is over for us. Too many dead. That's all I have to say," said Neubauer, stalking out of the pits. However, when three drivers were killed in the Tourist Trophy Race at Belfast, Mercedes remained in and swept the first three places.

Mercedes returned to competition only in December 1951, after an 11-year lapse, entering its blown three-litre prewar race car in the Argentine Grand Prix. The following year, Mercedes captured the major races—Le Mans, Mexico, the Mille Miglia, and the Nurburg Ring. In 1953 Mercedes sat it out, and spent the year retooling for its $2\frac{1}{2}$ litre unsupercharged racer under the new Grand Prix formula. The unprecedented series of wins that followed in 1954-55 are well known.

Nevertheless, production of the 2½-litre racing car at Mercedes has halted. "We've gotten everything out of it that we can," said Neubauer. To admit to having reached the limts of racing-car development sounds a boast. But coming from Neubauer it is a simple fact of engineering.

"Next year," he added, "our Grand Prix cars might be a bit quicker, but not much—we've about hit the maximum. Any forward steps would be small in relation to the effort. So we're going to sports car production."

Neubauer is now eligible for retirement. It has been rumored he pushed for abandonment of racing car production as a personal end. Neubauer has after all captained history's classic racing team and established the superiority of German cars for his time. He might well like to burn behind him the bridges that led to his fame.

But not even Neubauer's enemies accept this. Friends and critics alike have come to see Neubauer instead as the last of a breed. Like a trumpeting king elephant who dominates the field, Neubauer hovers over the racing scene, his priority unquestioned.

14. The Man From Down-Under
by Dennis May

The Formula One Cooper is, as such machines go, a light car but to Jack Brabham on a particular day in December, 1959, the Cooper felt as heavy as a Berliet truck. For one thing, Jack was tired. He had led the first Grand Prix of the United States, except for five laps at the beginning, almost from wire to wire. For another thing, Jack was no longer driving—he was pushing. Trudging step after trudging step he had forced the dark green car along the Sebring course for three-quarters of a mile. It wasn't that he could win the race by pushing—his team-mate Bruce McLaren had already done that and through sweat-hazed eyes Jack could see the crowd surrounding the young New Zealander at the finish line. Still, he continued to push, desperately doing his utmost to get the Cooper across the line and, in so doing, finish the race. Finally, and except for the last few hundred feet almost unnoticed, Jack forced the crippled car over the line and then collapsed to the pavement.

He hadn't won the race he had led so long, but he finished it. That was the important thing for more was at stake than a single race. At the end of that long, staggering trudge, Jack Brabham became the 1959 Driving Champion of the World.

That last desperate shove to the championship didn't just begin on the back stretch at Sebring. It started thousands of miles away in Sydney, Australia. Dennis May, who knows Brabham as well as any "Pommie" could, tells how that push began and how the 1959 World Champion came to be.

"If Jack could just unlearn that village-blacksmith corner-ing technique of his and get himself some decent equipment, a few people would have to watch out." The fortune teller was Peter Collins, the date 1956, the place Aintree, the village blacksmith Jack Brabham, horny-handed son of a Sydney greengrocer.

Collins, killed in August of 1958, lived to see Brabham turn over a new stylistic leaf, earn a place on the Cooper works team and shape course for his subsequent win in the *Autocar's* seasonal Formula 2 championship. In '59, following outright wins in the grands prix of Monaco and Great Britain, second place at Zandvoort, thirds at Rheims and Monza, he topped the table for the World Championship with only the U.S. Grand Prix to go.

Having led the scoring uninterruptedly throughout the European season, Jack had had ample time, pre-Sebring, to marshal his philosophy relative to the championship. Nat-urally he'd be pleased if he won but, like Tony Brooks, he had never lost a wink of sleep as his chances alternately soared and steadied. Whoever else was troubled with insomnia on the night of December 11, it wasn't this graduate from the New South Wales dirt tracks. Commercially, nobody could be in-different to success in such a league; Jack, having recently set himself up in an auto dealership on the outskirts of Sur-biton, Cooper's hometown in Surrey, England, is well situated to translate kudos into pounds sterling. But the limelight that goes with the title is a bore, a bane and an embarrassment to him.

Such is the man's artless honesty that nobody who knows him doubts his sincerity in avowing this. Invitations to make speeches at motor club dinners, write magazine articles, hold still for newspaper interviews, endorse products ranging from jockstraps to Judo courses, appear on television, talk on radio: "It's getting to be terrible already, really terrible," he told us before Sebring. "I dread what it'll be like if we win the championship."

The Brabham smile is constant and infectious.

These sentiments, you may think, will be hard to reconcile with the publication of a Jack Brabham autobiography that's in course of preparation. The explanation is this: if authorship committed him to sitting down at a typewriter, or wielding a pen, the book would never have gotten as far as the title page. It doesn't, though. Monosyllabic in public, and in company he doesn't know well, Jack has a surprising muzzle velocity when the mood is on him and he's among close friends, most of whom are Australians. Such a one is Dev Dvoretsky of the London bureau of Australian Consolidated Press. Literary collaborator as well as bosom companion, Dev haunts Brabham's slipstream from Aintree to Avus, finger on the trigger of his tape recorder in readiness for signs that the driver is about to turn on the verbal faucet.

Although by no means ill disposed towards Pommies (Australian for the English) as a race, Brabham has a tendency, which he feels he ought to resist in his own interest, to surround himself in exile with Australasians. His personal mechanic, Tim Wall, formerly with Rob Walker on the Pippbrook stable, is an Aussie. (The F-2 Cooper-Climax that Jack ran during 1959 is his own property, which is why he needs a racing mechanic of his own.) His manager at the Triumph Rootes agency, Phil Kerr, is from New Zealand. Jack's wife, Betty, is Australian, and their eight year old son, Geoff, was born in Australia. Try to reach Jack on the 'phone and the voice that answers you, nine times out of ten, will identify the speaker with Brabham's household brigade of Antipodeans.

Since Mike Hawthorn was killed, I'd say Jack's personal popularity was unsurpassed among British and Commonwealth drivers of the top class, and probably only equalled by Tony Brooks. About the only dissenters from the we-love-Jack chorus are English racing mechanics, whom Brabham, with native frankness, once compared unfavorably with their Australian counterparts in a magazine article.

Since the demise of the prewar tradition that cast the supposedly typical British racing driver for the role of a hard drinking heathen, devoted to polygamy in picturesque forms and creating disturbances while in liquor, the barometer of conduct in this sector of society has counterswung to an almost monotonous reading of Blameless. Brabham, it's our duty to record, runs true to modern type. As a constant foil for the unique brand of wit that marks John Cooper as the four-star comedian of the English and continental racing scene, Jack has abundant scope for the viceless horsing that comes naturally to him, but it goes no further than that. His humor is never unkind and its target is often Jack Brabham. He doesn't smoke, doesn't drink. "I gave 'em both up when I left school." An affectionate father, he returns from every foreign racing sortie laden like Santa Claus with gifts for his kid. Sometimes these are so bulky he has trouble persuading the airline to accept them as personal baggage. Betty Brabham accompanies Jack to most of his races, abroad as well as in Britain, and looks after his timekeeping for him.

For the record, in chronological order, here's where and how Brabham amassed his pre-Sebring total of 31 points in the 1959 World Championship:—

Monaco GP: First, at 66.74 mph, ahead of Brooks (Ferrari) and Trintignant (Rob Walker's Cooper-Climax); also fastest lap at 70.09 mph and first-ever race laps at above seventy. 9 points.

Netherlands GP, Zandvoort: Second, 14.2 seconds behind Bonnier (BRM) and 1'8.8" ahead of his Cooper works team mate, Masten Gregory. 6 points.

French GP (GP d'Europe), Rheims: Third, way behind Brooks and Phil Hill. 4 points.

British GP, Aintree: First, 22.2 seconds in front of Moss (BRM) and followed by Bruce McLaren, number three on the Cooper team and Jack's personal protege. 8 points.

German GP, Avus: Brabham broke his clutch in the first heat, didn't start in the second. No take.

Portuguese GP, Monsanto: Crashed. No take.

Italian GP, Monza: Third, behind Moss (Cooper-Climax) and Phil Hill (Ferrari); 25.8 seconds down on Hill. 4 points.

To anyone who follows the grand prix circus intelligently, even vicariously through the race reports of such knowing writers as *SCI's* Jesse Alexander, the London *Motor's* Rodney Walkerley, *Autocar's* Peter Garnier and *Motor Sport's* Denis Jenkinson, it's obvious Jack Brabham is not the best road race driver in the world, even as 1959 World Champion, and he'll be the last to deny it. But in England in particular, in the eyes of a million or two cursorily interested followers of the sport who base their opinions on grand prix reports in popular newspapers, Jack's rating has suffered indirectly and unfairly at the hands of a specter known as the Moss Jinx. Having conjured this genie out of its bottle of printer's ink, its creators plug it to a degree that's become purely ridiculous. If Moss wins, God's in His heaven and all's well with the World Championship; if he loses, *cherchez la* Jinx. In races that have been won by British or Commonwealth drivers other than Moss, this ubiquitous and iniquitous Jinx has often hogged the headlines to the exclusion of the winner's exploit.

If and when Brabham (for instance) crashes or blows up through no fault of his own, the glamor-drunk scribes of the lay press don't pump *him* for the story of *his* hoodoo's latest treachery, for he doesn't have a hoodoo accredited to him. And because, as Smollett put it. "True courage scorns to vent her prowess in a storm of words," it's for sure the publicly reticent Aussie won't take the trouble to spell it all out for the reporters' benefit.

Granted, if everything had gone right for Stirling throughout '59, always, he'd have gone to Sebring with better than 25½ Championship points to his credit. By the same token, though, if everything had gone right for Brabham, *his* pre-Sebring total would have been better than 31. But let it be understood this interpretation of events is entirely our own, and not inspired by anything Jack says or even hints at. In matters of racing strategy and tactics, his thinking and Stirling's often have an uncanny similarity, and Jack is a sincere and overt admirer of Moss.

For practical proof of his feeling towards the man who was to chase him up the 1959 championship ladder, it's only necessary to recall an act of Samaritanism during the New Zealand GP meeting at Ardmore last January. In his heat, Moss broke one of his Cooper's halfshafts and suspension

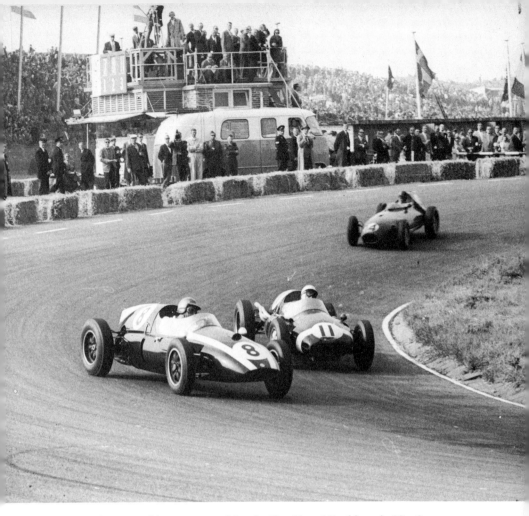

Two methods of taking a corner—Moss in No. 11 and Brabham in No. 8.

units. The mangled parts were beyond local repair and, having
no replacements of his own, it seemed he'd have to sit the
final out. Brabham had replacements, though, and unhesi-
tatingly came across with them. Stirling won the final, Jack
placed second.

You'd hardly think a catalog of if's and but's, relative
to Brabham's 1959 Championship progression, would need
to include the Monaco GP; he won the race, after all, and
also broke the lap record, and you can't do much better than
that. Well, not *much* better, maybe, but in fact, if it hadn't
been for a transmission derangement which, as far as we

know, hasn't hitherto been mentioned anywhere in print, he might well have made it a 100 per cent score by beating Maurice Trintignant's 1958 race record of 67.98 mph. At around half distance, bottom gear on Jack's Cooper started jumping out. Thereafter he only used low briefly and inter-mittently, when Brooks was leaning on him unbearably. Preeminently, of course, the Monaco circuit, shortest and slowest of the *grande epreuve* venues, is a place where it really hurts to be bereft of bottom cog, with the alternative of driving one-handedly to hold it in. Nonetheless, it was as late as lap 85, fifteen from the finish, that Brabham set his terrific 70.09 mph lap record.

In the second title round at Zandvoort three weeks later, he'd no sooner taken the lead from Jo Bonnier (BRM) on the thirtieth lap when his second gear went up the spout. That left 45 laps to race with an excruciatingly wide ratio box. So it was legitimate for Brabham apologists to speculate whether, if this hadn't happened, Bonnier would later have passed (to win), or Moss would have passed (to retire twelve laps from the end with malfunction of his Cooper's Colotti gearbox).

Jack's third placement in the European Grand Prix at Rheims, where the Ferraris of Tony Brooks and Phil Hill headed him, calls for no excuses or qualifying clauses: except perhaps to fill in a gap in the contemporary reports—even the good ones—by saying the reason why Brabham surrendered second place to Hill at around lap 26 was that Jack's clutch had started slipping. The shortage of friction persisted for ten or fifteen rounds.

During practice at Rheims, Cooper tried out their aero-dynamic body on both of Jack's cars—the works FI machine and his own 1½-liter that he ran in the F2 race. This shell, with a sawed-off tail based on Kamm principles, gave the full grand prix contender a top speed of around 190 mph on the straight, but it was also indirectly responsible for Jack's re-tirement in the F2 contest, despite the fact it was replaced by an open-wheel body before either race came off. The reason was simply that the lack of brake ventilation during training had given the smaller car's brakes such a cooking they wouldn't stand up to the race session.

A secondary reason for his F2 defection was that, under the hottest race conditions ever recorded in a European classic—ambient temperature 95 degrees F, surface temperature 190F—Brabham became as badly detuned physically as anyone in the act. Even in Australian races, he'd never had it that hot. Like most of the rest, he suffered his share of face lacerations from stones thrown up from the molten road surface.

The Brabham hoodoo (if you're prepared to admit the existence of this poor relation of the Moss Jinx) took furlough from spite the day of the British GP at Aintree, championship round four. With the works Ferraris absent due to industrial trouble in Italy, Jack led from start to finish with hardly a care in the world apart from worrying whether his tires would last out (he went through nonstop).

Round five, of course, was the farcical German GP along the dreary flats and near-suicidal Nordkurve of the Avus— a Ferrari benefit as far as it benefitted anyone. Brabham, as recalled earlier, killed his clutch in the first heat and nonstarted in the second. It certainly isn't sour grapes that prompts him to declare he'd never again submit car and person to this sort of Roman holiday, because the successful Ferrari team men were of the same mind.

But there were bigger scares in store for Jack, who doesn't scare easily, three weeks away in Portugal. First he had to dodge a child who pitterpattered across his Cooper's bows at 125 an hour (this was the Cooper's speed, not the child's); then a jaywalking official forced Brabham into another phenomenal avoidance; finally, when lying second to Moss and all set for six vital points, he was involved in the first really bad crash of his career. He was blamed for this accident by normally perspicacious British reporters, none of whom, it's relevant to add, actually witnessed it. In fact, by our interpretation, his only fault was that, not being clairvoyant, he failed to foresee that a Portuguese driver, Cabral (Cooper-Maserati) would suddenly change his line on a corner when Jack, coming up fast from behind, was too far committed to play it contrapuntal.

The fact that Cabral was driving for the experienced Scuderia Centro-Sud made it presumable he knew what he was doing. Brabham's car hit a telegraph pole and threw him out. As he landed he just missed being flattened by Masten Gregory's works Cooper, which finally placed second to Moss on Rob Walker's Cooper-Climax entry.

Expectedly, in view of preceding revelations, the story of Brabham's bid for the Italian Grand Prix yields a significant now-it-can-be-told item. Cooper had had special gears made up in advance for Monza. During practice, however, due to a fault in heat treatment, their teeth started coming out in handfuls, forcing the team to fall back on cogs giving painfully low ratios for this very fast circuit (lap record by Phil Hill, Ferrari, 128.12 mph). Speed for speed in top, Jack's rpm was 500 up on the planned turnover, and the same went for his team mates, McLaren and Scarlatti. So it's fair to comment that Jack, who finished third behind Moss on the Walker stable's Cooper-Climax and Phil Hill (Ferrari), not only did well to make his tires last the 259 mile race distance (which Stirling also did but the Ferrari team didn't), but furthermore nursed his overrevved engine through without mishap.

By common consensus, Brabham's selftaught knowledge and skill as an engineer start where that of most of his grand prix contemporaries leaves off. Knowing cars as he knows them, and never racing one he hasn't worked on with his own hands (sports cars excepted) is, he considers, a double-edged asset. On the one hand, enabling him to foresense impending

The Cooper team, left to right: Brabham, Bruce McLaren, John Cooper.

crackups, it can be the means of turning a probable retirement into a lame finish—which is better than no finish where championship points are at stake. On the other hand, in the same situation, a less sensitive operator will keep his clog down and conceivably bash through a high placement. It doesn't always pay, in other words, to know the worst that may happen.

Brabham is the first Champion in history with the distinction of having built and played an important part in the development of the cars he races. He could be classified as the polar opposite of the late Fon Portago, who was about as much use in a workshop as a left handed gorilla and didn't even like cars much, and the approximate counterpart of the great and equally lamented Frank Lockhart. His gifts as an engineer were doubtlessly congenital, but he attributes their practical development to the fact that in Australia, back in his dirt track and hillclimb days, the business was so unprofitable he had no option but to be his own mechanic.

Things looked up a bit when Jack secured a Redex sponsorship for a road race program with the front-engined Cooper-Bristol he was operating in New South Wales and neighboring States in the early 'fifties. Then, at the end of 1954, the Confederation of Australian Motor Sport outlawed sponsorships, which was a contributing factor in Brabham's decision to go to England in '55—"just for one season." He was so sure the sojourn would be temporary he bought a building lot in Sydney with the firm intention of setting up there in a garage business. Little did he think his garage venture, when it finally materialized—five years later—would be located just down the road from Cooper Cars Ltd. at Surbiton, England.

Jack recently sold his piece of Sydney and, except for occasional trips to visit his father, isn't likely to be seeing much of Australia in the future. After Sebring he headed straight for New Zealand and the New Zealand Grand Prix in January.

Arriving in England in the spring of 1955, Jack acquired an out-of-breath Cooper-Alta from the late Peter Whitehead and, in the memorable Ustinov phrase, leapt into obscurity. Cars that followed, *chez* Brabham, included the old 250F Maserati with which the Alfred Owen stable used to console itself for the BRM's lack of success, but this one, in the village blacksmith's hands, never really regained the form it had shown when Peter Collins drove it to victory in the 1955 International *Daily Express* Trophy at Silverstone. It was in

1956 that Brabham went onto the Cooper payroll, where, to shorten an intractably long story, he has been ever since. His between-race duties have included the bulk of Cooper's high speed testing and, in particular, improving and developing the cars' handling qualities. The Cooper firm has of course won the 1959 FI Constructors' World Championship by miles from Ferrari; so Jack also can justly adorn his hat with a few of the feathers that go with victory in the makers' contest.

We once overheard a Brands Hatch spectator say, in awestruck and admiring tones, "With Brabham you never know for sure which will come into sight first, his back wheels or the front ones." Transition from his old haymaker cornering modus came gradually, almost imperceptibly. Except for occasional lapses in the heat and fury of short races on dizzy courses like Brands Hatch, where almost everybody resorts to wild-fowling technique anyway, Jack's latterday style well deserved the adjectives "cool, immaculate," that *Autosport's* account of the 1959 British GP applied to it. He doesn't yet have the almost sculptured poise of Moss and Brooks at the wheel, because this would be impossible to combine with his habit of telescoping his neck into his shoulders to get himself down out of the airstream. But gone forever is the old brute-force touch that used to be such a delight to the Brabham fans of two continents.

In international FI races of sub-Championship caliber during 1959, Brabham and Moss were constantly in each other's hair, fighting a series of tigerish battles. Coincidentally, the first and the last of these, the Goodwood 100-miler at Easter and the Oulton Park Gold Cup race in September, had the same outcome—Stirling first, Jack second. In the latter, for the biggest first prize purse of any current British race (1000 pounds, nearly $3000), Brabham became a figure of controversy over what appeared to be a deliberate and blatant jumped start. Because nobody bothered to ask him what gave, and he, characteristically, didn't bother to tell anyone, the impression remained that Jack had momentarily reverted to blacksmith type. The fact was, and it only emerged under our crossquestioning, that Cooper had been experimenting with a new type of clutch, giving a shortened pedal travel. When Brabham realized, all in a split second, he was the only one racing for the Gold Cup, he hit his brakes hard, risking a shunt up the bustle in so doing. In the general brouhaha, this act of reparation went unnoticed. Anyway, he wasn't complaining—he'd won the cup and the accompanying thousand sterling a couple of years earlier.

Brabham is not without experience as a sports-car driver but he's happier in the *vitesse pure* school. As a short-term member of the Aston Martin works team in '58 he co-drove the winning DBRI-300 with Moss in the Nurburgring 1000-Kilometers, and shared Roy Salvadori's second place in the TT. It's been written that he is the only Australian ever to finish at Le Mans, but this should read the only Australian *male;* Joan Richmond, Aussie *aussi,* placed high in her Le Mans class when Jack was still in short pants.

In '59 his sports car program was confined to the sideshow contest for this class of car in the British GP meeting, where he was third, and the TT at Goodwood, where he retired on Monaco Coopers both times. His best "week's" work during 1959, to revert to FI level, was winning the Silverstone International one Saturday and the Monaco GP eight days later. No doubt the shade of Peter Collins nodded approval of Jack's new-found tidiness in averaging 102.73 mph to win the Silverstone annual. Back when Peter himself won it, at 95.94 mph on the Owen Maserati in 1955, it could have seemed that the Australian never would snap out of that village blacksmith technique.